ZION NATIONAL PARK
THE COMPLETE GUIDE

2nd Edition

©2023 DESTINATION PRESS & ITS LICENSORS
ISBN: 978-1-940754-52-9

Written, Photographed and Illustrated by James Kaiser

Special thanks to all the National Park Service employees who helped me with this book, particularly Mike Large, Erin Whittaker, Miriam Watson, Penelope Yocum, and Kevin Wheeler. You were all incredibly generous with your time. Keep up the good work! Thanks also to local gurus Geoffrey Gerstner, Jess Kavanaugh, and Rick Praetzel, who all taught me things about Zion I didn't know.

Thank you to my family, friends, and all those who supported me while working on this guidebook. Thank you to the Himoff family (Adam, Andrea, Isabel, Madeline) and Aaron Geer and his family. And above all thank you to my wonderful wife Andrea Rincon , who hiked, biked, backpacked, camped and canyoneered—all while looking lovely.

All information in this guide has been exhaustively researched, but names, phone numbers, and other details do change. If you encounter a change or mistake while using this guide, please send an email to changes@jameskaiser.com. Your input will help make future editions of this guide even better. Special thanks to eagle-eyed readers Kurt Sawitskas, Frank Petty, and Chris Slackway for finding errors in past editions.

Printed in Malaysia

ZION

NATIONAL PARK

THE COMPLETE GUIDE

2nd Edition

JAMES KAISER

CONGRATULATIONS!

IF YOU'VE PICKED UP this book, you're going to Zion. Perhaps you're already here. If so, you're in one of America's most spectacular national parks—a remarkable landscape filled with stunning geology and world-class outdoor adventures.

When I first visited Zion, a familiar sensation took hold. The towering cliffs, lush vegetation and cool springs reminded me of gorgeous canyons I had visited at the bottom of Grand Canyon. Those hidden cathedrals—some of the most beautiful places in the Southwest—take days to reach by river or trail. But in Zion you can experience similar scenery in a leisurely afternoon. You don't need to be an expert in rafting or rappelling to enjoy the beauty of Zion. In fact, some of the park's best destinations are also some of the most accessible.

Standing on the floor of Zion Canyon, surrounded by 2,000-foot cliffs, it's easy to be impressed by the landscape. But take some time to learn the story behind the scenery, and Zion becomes even more amazing. With some basic ecology, tiny springs blossom into nourishing oases filled with fascinating plants and animals. With some basic geology, sandstone cliffs become 200-million-year-old sand dunes—compacted, solidified and sliced open for your viewing pleasure.

Early settler David Flanigan once wrote that in Zion "one may look, listen, see, hear, feel, and think, and live a thousand years in a day." Your first day in Zion is a day you will never forget. But venture beyond the basics and you'll be rewarded a thousand times over.

With a limited amount of time, however, you've got to plan your trip wisely. This book puts the best of Zion at your fingertips. Whether you're here for rugged adventures or simply to marvel at the scenery, *Zion: The Complete Guide* is the only guide you'll need.

CONTENTS

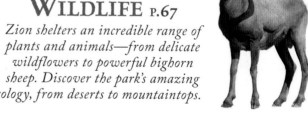

ZION CANYON P.127

One of America's most beautiful places, Zion Canyon is the crown jewel of the park—home to towering cliffs, narrow slot canyons, and Zion's most famous outdoor adventures.

EAST ZION P.215

Situated high above Zion Canyon, the road through East Zion twists and turns through a rolling sandstone wonderland that's as strange and fascinating as it is gorgeous.

KOLOB TERRACE P.249

Rising from the Mojave Desert to the highest viewpoint in the park, Kolob Terrace Road passes through stunning alpine scenery and provides access to some of the best hikes in the park.

KOLOB CANYONS P.273

Located in Zion's lonely northwest corner, Kolob Canyons boasts sheer sandstone cliffs and a beautiful scenic drive, with a fraction of Zion Canyon's crowds.

SOUTHWEST DESERT P.273

Zion's most overlooked region offers surprisingly beautiful desert hiking with sweeping views of the rugged landscapes just outside the park.

ZION TOP 5

TOP 5 VIEWPOINTS

TOP 5 ADVENTURES

TOP 5 EASY HIKES

TOP 5 HARD HIKES

Temple of Sinawava

The Narrows

INTRODUCTION

LOCATED IN SOUTHWEST Utah, Zion is a small park filled with big adventures. Sculpted by the Virgin River over the past two million years, Zion Canyon shelters some of America's most incredible scenery. Sheer cliffs tower above narrow slot canyons, dramatic hiking trails rise to panoramic viewpoints, and unlikely springs nourish cool, lush oases. It's as if Mother Nature gathered everything lovely about the desert Southwest and placed it into a single, scenic masterpiece.

Radiating out from Zion Canyon are additional marvels. East Zion is a sprawling expanse of wavy sandstone, easily explored along a 10-mile road. Southwest Zion marks the northeast fringe of the Mojave Desert, which is home to amazing plants and animals. To the west, Kolob Terrace Road rises through bold canyons into an alpine forest of aspen and pine—a landscape more like the Rockies than the desert Southwest. And Zion's most remote destination, Kolob Canyons, is a rugged outpost with towering rock spires, gorgeous hiking trails, and one of the world's largest free-standing rock arches.

All this natural beauty is made possible by Zion's geology. Over the past 300 million years, Zion has hosted a head-spinning variety of unlikely environments, including tropical seas, sand dune deserts, lakes, rivers and swamps. Each laid down a new layer of eroded sediments, which were ultimately buried and compressed into sedimentary rocks. Tectonic forces pushed these rock layers thousands of feet above sea level, and rivers carved through the scenery to create Zion's legendary canyons and cliffs.

At 230 square miles, Zion National Park is just one-eighth the size of Grand Canyon. Although relatively small, the park's wrinkled topography is a natural jungle gym that lures outdoor junkies from around the world. Easy day hikes and multi-day backpacks crisscross the park, opening up hidden alcoves and forested plateaus. Biking is a great way to explore Zion Canyon, and rock climbers enjoy some of America's most accessible big walls. Perhaps most extraordinary is Zion's world-class canyoneering. Dozens of narrow canyons slice through the park, luring canyoneers who hike, scramble, swim and rappel through the psychedelic slots. You could easily spend a month in Zion and not run out of things to do. So let's get started!

Trail

HIKING

H<small>IKING IS ONE</small> of the best ways to experience Zion. Nothing puts the landscape in perspective like time on the trail, getting up close and personal with the park's fabulous geology. From mellow strolls along the Virgin River to hair-raising scrambles up rocky peaks, there's a hike for every age and ability. Don't sell yourself short by hanging around Zion's parking areas and shuttle stops. The more physical effort you put in, the more you'll be rewarded.

The park's most popular hikes are in Zion Canyon, where a handful of trails zigzag up sheer cliffs to fabulous viewpoints. The most dramatic is Angels Landing (p.174), which requires navigating a thin rocky ledge with thousand-foot dropoffs—one of the most harrowing trails in America. Observation Point (p.204) rises 2,000 feet above the northern end of Zion Canyon to a gorgeous panorama, and Hidden Canyon (p.208) explores a beautiful slot canyon half-way up the cliffs. Zion Canyon's most famous hike, however, is a splashy stroll through The Narrows (p.184), a dramatic slot canyon where the "trail" is the Virgin River. Less demanding hikes include the Pa'rus Trail (p.134), Emerald Pools (p.150), Weeping Rock (p.158) and Riverside Walk (p.169).

If there's a downside to Zion Canyon trails it's crowds during peak season. Fortunately, there are plenty of terrific hikes in higher, cooler, less crowded parts of the park. Kolob Terrace is home to The Subway (p.256), whose ethereal contours lure photographers from around the world, and Northgate Peaks(p.266), one of the best easy hikes in the park. Hop Valley (p.268) and West Rim Trail (p.260) are longer trails enjoyed by both hikers and backpackers.

East Zion's most popular trail is Canyon Overlook (p.223), a moderate hike to a spectacular viewpoint. There are also a handful of "unofficial" trails off the main road such as Many Pools (p.226) and Progeny Peak (p.224). Several trails also start near the boundary of East Zion and lead to wonderful viewpoints along Zion Canyon's east rim, including Cable Mountain (p.232), Deertrap Mountain (p.236), and an easy shortcut to Observation Point.

Kolob Canyons, located in Zion's remote northwest corner, is a great place to escape the crowds in summer, with nice trails at Timber Creek Overlook (p.277) and Taylor Creek Trail (p.280). For a more challenging hike or backpack, check out the La Verkin Creek Trail (p.282), which passes by Zion's largest free-standing rock arch. Finally, Zion's lowest, warmest region is the Southwest Desert, where the Chinle Trail (p.246) is a great option during the cooler months.

Desert Hiking Tips

Hiking in southern Utah presents several challenges, most notably hot summer temperatures that can top 100°F in Zion Canyon. When temperatures spike, consider hiking in the cooler morning or evening hours. Another option is hiking in higher, cooler parts of the park such as Kolob Canyons, Kolob Terrace or East Zion. Always carry and drink plenty of water (rangers recommend one gallon per person, per day), and protect your skin from harmful UV rays with high SPF sunscreen and a wide-brimmed hat. To cool down, a wet bandanna on the back of the neck works wonders.

Trail Conditions

Current trail conditions and closures are posted on Zion's website (nps.gov/zion). Always check current conditions before you hike. The Wilderness Desk at the Zion Canyon Visitor Center is another great source for hiking information.

Hiking/Backpacking Permits

Permits are required to hike Angels Landing, The Subway, and for all backpacking trips. The park is also considering day hiking permits for some popular trails such as The Narrows, which have become extremely crowded in recent years. Check the park's website (nps.gov/zion) for current permit info.

ADVANCE PERMITS

Over half of all permits can be reserved on the park's website up to three months in advance. March permits become available January 5 at 10am MT, April permits become available February 5 at 10am MT, and so on. Cost: $5 online reservation fee plus $15–25 depending on group size.

WALK-IN PERMITS

About one-third of permits are reserved for walk-in permits and cannot be reserved in advance. Those permits become available at park visitor centers the day before a trip.

Hiking/Backpacking Shuttles

Some of Zion's popular hikes and backpacks start at remote trailheads. Unless you have two cars, transportation can be tricky. Fortunately, private shuttles can drop you off at popular trailheads. **Red Rock Shuttle & Tours** (435-635-9104, redrockshuttle.com) offers daily shuttle service with advance reservations; pickup is at the Zion Canyon Visitor Center. **Zion Adventure Company** (435-772-1001, zionadventures.com) offers daily shuttle service departing from its store in Springdale. Shuttle prices generally run $20-40 per person, depending on the . Large groups can sometimes negotiate a discount.

Zion's Best Hikes

Zion Canyon

Angels Landing

East Zion

Canyon Overlook

Kolob Terrace

Northgate Peaks

Kolob Canyons

The Subway

Southwest Desert

Flash Floods

Flash floods are one of Zion's greatest dangers. During monsoon season—July, August, September—powerful thunderstorms sweep through the region (p.35). Storms can dump several inches of rain in just a few hours, and the rocky, sun-baked landscape does little to absorb the water or slow it down. Runoff channels into narrow side canyons, forming flash floods that can reach speeds topping 23 feet *per second*, ripping out trees and vegetation and tumbling boulders like ice cubes. Perhaps most frightening, flash floods can happen when skies are sunny and clear overhead. If a thunderstorm several miles distant dumps rain over a canyon's headwaters, a flash flood can roar downstream, catching unsuspecting hikers and canyoneers by surprise. The wall of water often moves so fast that it ___es the air in front, sending pebbles and small rocks flying through the ___ u find yourself in the path of a flash flood, climb as high as you can as

quickly as possible. It is not possible to outrun or outswim a flash flood. Even if you are only a few feet above the water, those few feet can save your life. If there is no high ground, seek shelter behind a large rock that can break the wall of oncoming water. Squeezing into a crack or crevice along a rock wall is another last-ditch option.

The best way to avoid flash floods is to stay away from narrow canyons when the forecast calls for rain. Zion posts weather forecasts at all park entrances and visitor centers, and flash flood alerts are posted on Twitter (@ZionNPS). Flash flood alerts, which are issued by the National Weather Service, prompt the closure of The Narrows and other potentially dangerous trails.

Canyoneers, who seek out narrow canyons, face the greatest danger from flash floods. When picking up canyoneering permits, ask about the weather. If a park ranger suggests staying away from certain canyons, heed the advice. Canyoneers who disregard ranger warnings have died in flash floods.

West Rim Trail

BACKPACKING

BACKPACKING IS MORE challenging than hiking, but the rewards are even greater. If you're willing to strap on an overnight backpack filled with camping gear and food, you can access some of Zion's most glorious, uncrowded landscapes. There's nothing like finishing a full day of hiking at a beautiful campsite surrounded by wilderness, then falling asleep under a blanket of stars.

There are about half a dozen popular backpacking trails in Zion, most of which explore the high elevations above Zion Canyon. This alpine wilderness is home to lush meadows and pine forests that often feature dramatic views of the canyons below. One of Zion's best backpacks is the West Rim Trail (p.260), which starts near Lava Point, traverses a high plateau with campsites on the rim, then drops into Zion Canyon. Another great option is the East Rim Trail (p.238), which starts in East Zion, climbs to a ponderosa forest with side trails leading to fabulous viewpoints, then drops into Zion Canyon along the Observation Point Trail.

Northwest Zion is another backpacking hotspot. The Hop Valley Trail (p.268) starts in Kolob Terrace and descends towards Kolob Canyons. It connects with the La Verkin Creek Trail (p.282), where a dozen campsites are spread along a beautiful creek that wraps around Kolob Canyons' towering buttes. When winter snow covers Zion's high elevations, backpackers enjoy the Chinle Trail (p.246), which explores the park's warmer, low elevation desert.

Zion's most unique backpack, however, is The Narrows (top-down) (p.196). Unlike The Narrows bottom-up, which is crowded with day hikers, The Narrows top-down passes through The Narrows' remote upper section, which requires a permit to enter. Twelve campsites are scattered along the upper Narrows, offering solitude and privacy that's completely absent from the lower Narrows.

Most Zion backpacks can be done in two days. If you're hungry for more, consider the Trans-Zion Trek, which links six trails (La Verkin, Hop Valley, Connector Trail, Wildcat Canyon, West Rim, East Rim) to create a 47-mile backpack across the entire park that takes 3–5 days.

All backpacks in Zion require permits (p.14), which are in high demand during peak season. If you can't reserve a permit in advance, stop by the Wilderness Desk when you arrive and ask which trails have last-minute "walk-in" permits available. The Wilderness Desk also posts vital information, such as which springs are currently flowing. Visit Zion's website (nps.gov/zion) for more information on backpacking safety and rules.

Pa'rus Trail

BIKING

EACH YEAR IT seems like Zion Canyon's shuttle lines grow a little bit longer, the riders a little more restless. But there's one group of savvy visitors who just don't care: bicycle riders. While dozens, sometimes *hundreds* of shuttle riders line up like sheep, bicyclists are peddling through Zion Canyon, enjoying 360-degree open-air views of the park's magnificent scenery.

The adventure begins on the Pa'rus Trail (p.134), which starts near the Zion Canyon Visitor Center. Bicyclists are allowed on the Pa'rus Trail, which follows the Virgin River 1.8 miles upstream to Canyon Junction. From Canyon Junction you'll follow Zion Canyon Scenic Drive six miles up Zion Canyon. Because Zion Canyon Scenic Drive is closed to private vehicles when shuttles are running, shuttles are generally the only traffic you'll encounter. Shuttles are not allowed to pass moving bicycles, so when a shuttle approaches in your lane pull over to a complete stop on the side of the road.

Biking in Zion Canyon is relatively easy with just a few uphill sections. If you'd rather not sweat, all Zion shuttles are equipped with bike racks that can hold at least two bikes, which means you can ride the shuttle past challenging sections—most notably the 2.5-mile uphill stretch between Canyon Junction and Zion Lodge. Another option is riding the shuttle to its final stop at the Temple of Sinawava, then pedaling (mostly) downhill back to the park entrance. (The 3-mile stretch between the Temple of Sinawava and The Grotto includes a few ups and downs.)

Bicycle rentals are available from several Springdale outfitters (p.45), including Zion Cycles, Zion Outfitter, and Zion Adventure Company. Springdale has dedicated bike lanes to safely bike across town. Zion Lodge (p.148) also rents bicycles in the heart of Zion Canyon. Bicycle rental rates generally run about $25 for a half day, $35 for a full day. Unless you rent from Zion Lodge, you'll want the full day to explore Zion Canyon without rushing.

Bicyclists are allowed on all paved roads in Zion, but bicyclists are not allowed through Zion Tunnel, which separates East Zion from Zion Canyon. Mountain biking is prohibited in Zion, but there are several good trails just outside the park, including the JEM trail and Gooseberry Mesa. Zion Cycle and Zion Adventure Company both offer mountain biking tours. In October the Red Bull Rampage, an extreme mountain biking competition, is held just outside the park.

Keyhole Canyon

CANYONEERING

DOZENS OF NARROW slot canyons slice through the Navajo Sandstone in Zion. These canyons, sculpted by flash floods over millennia, shelter some of the Southwest's most spectacular scenery—serpentine cathedrals of stone and light, warped and dissolved into psychedelic contours. Although a few of these twisted temples are accessible to hikers—The Narrows (p.184), The Subway (p.256), Hidden Canyon (p.208)—most are the exclusive domain of canyoneers.

Canyoneering is the art and science of descending rugged canyons through a combination of hiking, scrambling, climbing, swimming and rappelling. It's a challenging, technical sport with breathtaking visual rewards. Though practiced around the world, southern Utah is one of the world's top canyoneering destinations due to its unique geology, balmy climate and thriving outdoor culture. It was here, in the late 1970s, that rock climbers first started using their gear to go down instead of up, opening mysterious new realms and giving birth to an entirely new sport.

Over the past two decades, canyoneering has exploded in popularity. What was once a fringe activity has gone mainstream, particularly in Zion, which is home to some of Utah's most incredible and accessible slot canyons. Although guided canyoneering is not allowed in the park, Springdale outfitters (p.45) such as Zion Adventure Company, Zion Guru and Zion Rock and Mountain Guides offer canyoneering instruction. Their classes, which last from one to three days, teach you canyoneering basics at easy canyons just outside the park. After successfully completing a class you should have the necessary skills to descend Zion's easier slot canyons on your own.

Canyoneering gear, which can be rented from local outfitters, includes ropes, harnesses, helmets, specialized boots, backpacks and wetsuits or dry suits. Why wetsuits or dry suits? Because even during the hottest summer months shady slot canyons can be chilly due to lack of sunlight. Combine cool ambient temperatures with frigid pools that require swimming and you have a recipe for hypothermia. Wetsuits and dry suits also protect you from cuts and scrapes.

All technical slot canyons in Zion require permits, which can be requested up to three months in advance on the park's website (nps.gov/zion). Last-minute walk-in permits are also available. The process is nearly identical to requesting hiking/backpacking permits (p.14) with two exceptions: permits for The

Subway and Mystery Canyon, which are so popular they are allocated by lottery. The park issues just 12 permits a day for some canyons, while other canyons have up to 60 permits a day. Maximum group size is limited to six. For current information on canyoneering permits and the lottery system visit Zion's website.

No matter which canyons you explore, always be aware of potential risks and dangers. When practiced properly canyoneering is very safe, but overconfidence and complacency quickly lead to trouble. There's a reason the majority of search and rescue operations in Zion are conducted for canyoneers. In addition to injuries from falling, flash floods (p.16) are one of the greatest dangers in slot canyons. Flash floods typically occur during monsoon season (p.35), but they can happen any time of year depending on the weather. Rangers at the Wilderness Desk are one of the best sources of current info on flash flood risks.

Canyoneering is a year-round activity in Zion, but some seasons are better than others. Spring has good temperatures and reduced crowds, but runoff from snowmelt can make some canyons dangerous. Summer is the busiest season, and hot temperatures bring relief to some normally frigid canyons, but flash floods during monsoon season from July to mid-September are a constant threat. Fall is one of best seasons for canyoneering due to nice temperatures, limited rain and reduced crowds. Winter is cold and icy, making it suitable only for those with advanced canyoneering experience.

Popular Canyons in Zion

Listed below are some of Zion's most popular canyons. A full canyoneering guide is beyond the scope of this book, but *Zion Canyoneering* by Tom Jones is a popular guidebook with over 40 technical canyoneering routes. Tom also runs the website canyoneeringusa.com, which is another good source of info.

KEYHOLE CANYON

The ultimate beginner canyon. Located in East Zion, Keyhole is perfect for those new to canyoneering. Time: 1–2 hours. Longest rappel: 30 feet.

PINE CREEK

Zion's most popular intermediate canyon, which starts in East Zion and drops down Pine Creek below Zion Tunnel. Time: 4–6 hours. Longest rappel: 100 feet.

THE SUBWAY

One of the most famous canyons in the park. From Kolob Terrace the route heads down the Left Fork of North Creek and drops into The Subway, one of the park's most beautiful landscapes. Time: 6–12 hours. Longest rappel: 30 feet.

MYSTERY CANYON

A favorite among experienced canyoneers, who consider it one of Zion's most spectacular canyons. The route finishes with a stunning, 120-foot rappel down Mystery Falls into The Narrows. Time: 5–8 hours. Longest rappel: 120 feet.

Angels Landing

ROCK CLIMBING

ZION IS HOME to some of the tallest sandstone cliffs in the world, which lure a steady stream of big wall rock climbers seeking routes 1,000 feet or higher. While Yosemite's soaring granite cliffs will always be America's Big Wall Mecca, Zion (aka "sandstone Yosemite") could easily be America's Big Wall Medina. Zion has hundreds of climbs between 800 and 1,500 feet, and a handful of climbs approaching 2,000 feet.

Of course, you don't have to climb thousands of feet to enjoy rock climbing in Zion. If you're new to climbing (or big wall sandstone), several Springdale outfitters (p.45) offer guided lessons. Zion Rock and Mountain Guides has a full service gear shop and specializes in climbing lessons for beginners and intermediates looking to improve their skills. Zion Adventure Company also offers guided climbing lessons, including classes geared towards families. Although guided rock climbing is not allowed in Zion, there are some great beginner and intermediate routes just outside the park.

No matter your skill level, rock climbers face unique challenges in Zion. Sandstone is loose and crumbly, which affects handholds, gear selection and gear placement. Also be aware that sandstone is weaker when wet, so use caution after rain or snow. The best conditions are from March to May and September to November. A full climbing guide is beyond the scope of this book, but *Zion Climbing Free and Clean* by Bryan Bird is a popular guidebook that covers over 250 climbing routes in the park.

When the painter Frederick Dellenbaugh (p.117) visited Zion in 1903, he noted that "Climbing, as a sport, can be carried on here with an unlimited field." In 1927 a daredevil climber named William Evans reached the summit of the Great White Throne, but Evans fell on descent, leading to a complicated rescue and a ban on rock climbing in Zion. Modern big wall rock climbing was pioneered in Yosemite in the 1950s and 60s, and in 1967 three Yosemite veterans (Fred Beckey, Pat Callis and Galen Rowell) convinced the park to let them climb the Great White Throne, which ushered in a new era of responsible rock climbing in Zion. The climbing ban was lifted, and Zion's most iconic routes were established in the 1970s. If you want to see what today's generation of rock stars are up to, head to Big Bend (p.164), which is surrounded by popular big walls.

Astronomy

In Zion light pollution is low, the air is dry, and the sky is powdered with stars. If you're not looking up at night, you're missing half the show. Zion rangers often offer free astronomy programs at Watchman Campground and Zion Lodge. The park's best stargazing, however, is at high-elevation areas such as Kolob Canyons, Kolob Terrace and East Zion. Look for the Pleaides while scanning the night sky. The Southern Paiute believe this seven-star constellation is a family of seven Paiutes who fled to the sky after a dispute with their father, Tu-rei-ris. When Tu-rei-ris saw them in the sky, he grew enraged and turned them into *pootsis* (stars). The family retaliated by turning Tu-rei-ris into a coyote. Even today, you can hear coyote howling at the stars to mourn his lost family.

ZION BASICS

Getting to Zion

Zion National Park is located about 160 miles northeast of Las Vegas, (3-hour drive) and about 330 miles south of Salt Lake City (5-hour drive). Las Vegas and Salt Lake City have the closest international airports. There's also a regional airport in St. George, Utah (40 miles west of Zion, 1-hour drive), serviced by commercial flights from Salt Lake City. Visit jameskaiser.com for detailed driving directions, including points of interest along the way.

Gateway Towns

Springdale, located just outside Zion's South Entrance, is the park's largest and most popular gateway town. See page 43 for detailed info on gateway towns.

Gas Stations

There are two gas stations in Springdale, but prices are about 25% higher than gas stations 20 miles west in Hurricane/La Verkin. The closest gas stations to East Zion are in Mount Carmel Junction, 13 miles east of East Entrance. Gas stations in Kanab, located 17 miles southeast of Mount Carmel Junction, are about 25% cheaper than Mount Carmel Junction.

Entrance Passes

A seven-day pass to Zion costs $35 per vehicle or family, $30 per motorcycle or $20 per pedestrian or bicyclists. Youth 15 and under are admitted free. Other options include the annual Zion Pass ($60) or the Interagency Annual Pass ($80), which gives you unlimited access to all U.S. national parks and federal recreation lands for one full year. You can purchase entrance passes at any entrance station.

Zion Entrance Stations

South Entrance

Located at the north end of Springdale, South Entrance is the park's most popular and crowded entrance. It provides quick access to the Zion Canyon Visitor Center (p.132), where the Zion Canyon Shuttle departs. South Entrance is actually two entrance stations: a vehicle entrance located on Route 9 and pedestrian entrance near Springdale shuttle stop #1.

East Entrance/Zion Tunnel

Far less congested than West Entrance, East Entrance welcomes those arriving from Bryce, Grand Canyon, Arches or Canyonlands. From the entrance station a 10-mile roads twists through East Zion (p.215), passes through the Zion Tunnel, and drops to Zion Canyon. Any vehicle 11' 4" feet high or higher, and any vehicle 7'10" wide or wider, must pay $15 for a permit and One Way Traffic Control Operation through the tunnel.

Kolob Canyons Entrance

Located just off Interstate 15 (exit 40), 40 miles from Springdale, this entrance provides access to Zion's beautiful yet overlooked Kolob Canyons (p.273).

Current Information

Entrance stations and visitor centers offer free information sheets with maps and seasonal info. Zion's website (nps.gov/zion) has a Current Conditions page with park alerts, trail closures, road conditions, weather forecasts and Virgin River flow rates. Zion's Twitter account (@ZionNPS) is a great source of current alerts.

Park Shuttles

Throughout much of the year, free shuttles depart from the Zion Canyon Visitor Center and loop between nine popular stops in Zion Canyon. When the shuttle is running, no private vehicles are allowed in Zion Canyon. A second shuttle system loops through nine popular stops in Springdale. The shuttles, which were introduced in 2000, have dramatically improved visitor experiences compared to the congested, polluted, road-ragey 1990s. Note: Shuttle service may be expanded in the future. Check the park website for current shuttle schedules.

Park Shuttle Tips

• From Memorial Day through September, Zion offers a free ranger-narrated shuttle tour that departs from the visitor center at 9am—with no line! Enjoy a 90-minute tour of the canyon, then ride the regular shuttle back at your leisure. Space is limited and reservations (required) are available up to three days in advance in person at the Zion Canyon Visitor Center information desk.

• Visit East Zion (p.215) or Kolob Terrace (p.249) in the morning, then explore Zion Canyon in the afternoon when the shuttle line is shorter.

• Hike the Pa'rus Trail (p.134) 1.8 miles to Canyon Junction (p.142), where the shuttle line is shorter.

• Rather than ride the shuttle, ride a bike into Zion Canyon (p.127). If you get tired, all shuttles are equipped with bike racks.

Parking

The Zion Canyon Visitor Center has a free parking area inside the park, but it often fills between 8 and 9am (sometimes sooner on popular weekends). Signs near the entrance indicate if the parking area is full. If spaces are available, park only in clearly established spaces. "Creative" parking can earn you a ticket and a tow. If no spaces are available, you'll need to park in Springdale.

The town of Springdale has over a thousand public and private parking spaces. Even if all parking spaces near the park entrance are full, there's generally plenty of parking throughout town, and Springdale's free shuttle can whisk you to the park entrance in minutes. Public parking spaces have hourly and daily rates, which can be paid by credit card (visit springdaletown.com for current parking rates, which vary by zone). Private parking lots in Springdale often charge $20 per day, but that rate can jump to $30 per day during busy weekends.

Parking is much easier to find in other parts of Zion National Park. During peak season and busy weekends, however, parking at popular trailheads can sometimes get tight.

Parking Tips

• Arrive early (6am in summer, 7am in spring and fall), ride the shuttle to Zion Lodge, and have breakfast at the Red Rock Grille. While others are looking for parking, you'll be dining in the heart of Zion Canyon.

• Explore East Zion (p.215), Kolob Terrace (p.249), or Kolob Canyons (p.273) in the morning, then visit Zion Canyon in mid- to late-afternoon after the Type A early birds have gone home. Note: The busier the season, the later in the afternoon parking spots open up at the Zion Canyon Visitor Center.

• Hoodoos General Store offers free all-day parking with a $20 purchase.

Restaurants in Zion

There are two restaurants in the park, both located at Zion Lodge (p.148).

RED ROCK GRILL $$$ (Breakfast, Lunch, Dinner)

Located on the second floor of Zion Lodge, this sit-down restaurant serves a nice variety of Western flavors with plenty of healthy options. Large windows frame impressive views of Zion Canyon. Dinner reservations required (435-772-7760). Breakfast 6:30am–10:30am; lunch 11:30am–3pm; dinner 5pm–10pm.

CASTLE DOME CAFÉ $$$ (Breakfast, Lunch, Dinner)

This seasonal snack bar on the first floor of Zion Lodge serves cafeteria-style burgers, hot dogs and fries, plus baked goods, coffee and espresso. Local craft beer is served on the outdoor patio.

Lodging in Zion

★ ZION LODGE

The only lodge in Zion is a rustic beauty situated in the heart of Zion Canyon. There are hotel rooms, deluxe suites, and (my personal favorite) rustic cabins with a small porch and a gas fireplace. During peak season, Zion Lodge is generally booked months in advance. (888-297-2757, zionlodge.com)

Lodging Outside Zion

Springdale and other gateway towns have dozens of hotels, inns and bed and breakfasts catering to Zion visitors. Rather than waste dozens of pages—when all you need is one hotel—I've posted all of my lodging recommendations online at jameskaiser.com/zion/hotels.

Camping in Zion

Zion National Park has three campgrounds: Watchman Campground and South Campground, located near the Zion Canyon Visitor Center, and Lava Point Campground, located in Kolob Terrace (p.249) roughly one-hour from Zion Canyon. Zion's campgrounds are *extremely* popular. Reserve your site as far in advance as possible at recreation.gov. Visit jameskaiser.com for campground photos and additional information.

★ WATCHMAN CAMPGROUND

Located just south of the Zion Canyon Visitor Center, Watchman Campground has 184 campsites, including 65 RV-only sites and 18 tent-only walk-in campsites. $20 per night ($30 with electricity). Reservations available six months in advance.

★ SOUTH CAMPGROUND

Located just north of Zion Canyon Visitor Center, South Campground has 117 campsites. $20 per night. Reservations available 14 days in advance.

LAVA POINT CAMPGROUND

Zion's only first-come, first-served campground has six primitive campsites at an elevation of 7,890 feet. Upside: no fee. Downside: no water.

Camping Outside Zion

There are roughly half a dozen camping options outside Zion National Park, ranging from relatively luxurious (hot showers, swimming pools) to spartan (camping on vacant Bureau of Land Management land). For a complete list of paid and free camping options outside the park, including photos and reservation tips, visit jameskaiser.com

When to Visit Zion

It's always a good time to visit Zion, but each season comes with its own set of pros and cons. Knowing what to expect will help you plan a great trip.

SPRING

Long days, pleasant weather and reduced crowds make spring a great time to visit Zion. Early spring (late March, April) can still be chilly, but snowmelt often forms beautiful waterfalls in Zion Canyon. The snowier the winter, the bigger the waterfalls. Unfortunately, big snow years can also limit high elevation hiking and keep The Narrows closed until June due to heavy runoff. May is one of my favorite months, filled with balmy temperatures and beautiful wildflowers. Memorial Day weekend (the busiest weekend of the year) heralds the arrival of big crowds and hot temperatures for the next several months.

SUMMER

Summer in Zion Canyon is hot and crowded, with long lines for shuttles and temperatures often topping 100°F. Book hotels and campsites as far in advance as possible. To escape the sweltering heat and tourist hordes in Zion Canyon, head to lesser known, higher elevation parts of the park like Kolob Terrace and Kolob Canyons, which are gorgeous in summer. Be aware that monsoon season, which brings regular afternoon thunderstorms, starts in July and can last through September. After Labor Day, crowds and temperatures drop, making September a wonderful month to visit Zion.

AUTUMN

Autumn is one of my favorite times to visit Zion due to comfortable temperatures, slightly reduced crowds, and—best of all—stunning foliage. In late September/early October daytime temperatures are often divine. Peak foliage starts in early October at the park's highest elevations, then shifts to progressively lower elevations over the next few weeks. Foliage in Zion Canyon peaks in late October/early November.

WINTER

Cold temperatures keep most visitors away during Zion's slowest season, but the park is never more beautiful than after a fresh dusting of snow. If you don't mind the cold, this is a great time to visit Zion. Nearly all of the park is open with the exception of Lava Point, which is often inaccessible due to deep snow. The biggest downsides to visiting in winter: limited outdoor adventures and ranger programs. The biggest upside to visiting in winter: private vehicles are allowed in Zion Canyon when the shuttle isn't running.

Weather & Climate

Zion's weather is heavily influenced by the North American Monsoon, which affects seasonal precipitation throughout the American Southwest. During the hottest months of the year—July through mid-September—the desert bakes under intense solar radiation. Hot air rises as fast as 50 feet per second, creating an area of low pressure that draws warm, humid air from the Gulf of California and the Gulf of Mexico. As the hot, humid air rises it comes into contact with cold, high-altitude air, forming enormous anvil-headed clouds that grow dark and ominous as they rise thousands of feet. Eventually the clouds burst, producing torrential afternoon thunderstorms. The storms generally dissipate by evening, and the next morning the cycle repeats itself. July through mid-September is called "monsoon season" in the Southwest, and flash floods (p.16) are a serious threat during this time. But the intensity of Zion's monsoon season varies from year to year. Zion is located on the North American Monsoon's western edge, which shifts annually, so some summers are extremely wet while others are unusually dry.

As temperatures cool in autumn, a new weather pattern takes hold. From November to March, prevailing winds arrive from the west, bringing moist air from the Pacific Ocean. Most of this moisture falls as snow on the Sierra Nevada Mountains, but some finds its way into southern Utah, where it falls as snow or rain in a mild, steady stream. Although winter storms are much less intense than summer storms, they can sometimes linger for days. Nearly half of Zion's precipitation falls between December and March.

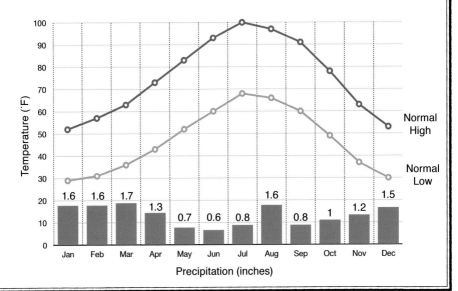

One Perfect Day in Zion

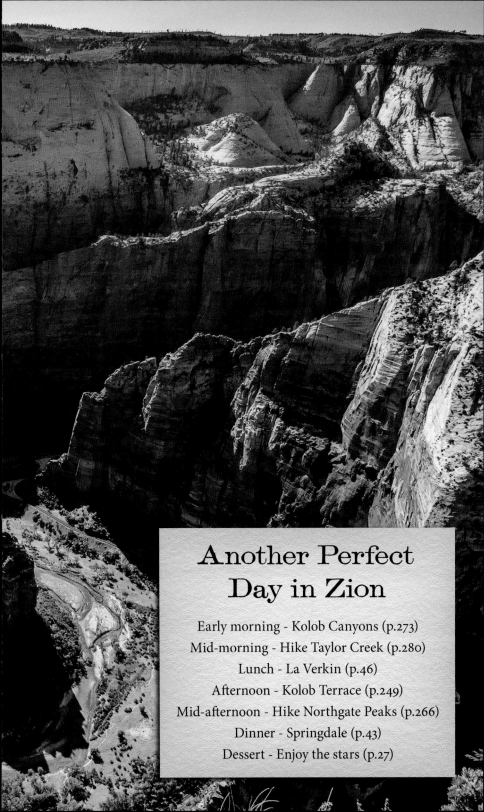

Another Perfect Day in Zion

Rainy Days in Zion

When first-time Zion visitors arrive during a rainstorm, they curse their bad luck. Meanwhile, locals and regulars are sprinting *into* the park. When a heavy rain hits Zion Canyon, dozens of spectacular waterfalls leap over the cliffs, creating America's most impressive and ephemeral liquid extravaganza. If you arrive when it's raining, consider yourself lucky. Anyone in Vegas can visit the Bellagio. Only a select few get to enjoy The Fountains of Zion. During peak runoff, water bursts out of every crevice, tumbling hundreds or even thousands of feet. You can enjoy the spectacle from the comfort of the shuttle, or put on your rain jacket and venture along the trails. No matter how you experience it, waterfall chasing in Zion is not to be missed. The most impressive waterfalls form at Emerald Pools (p.150), the Temple of Sinawava (p.167), Weeping Rock (p.158) and the Court of the Patriarchs (p.146).

Birch Creek Falls

Ranger Programs

Free ranger programs are offered from mid-April to mid-October, and they are one of the best ways to learn about Zion. Knowledgeable rangers discuss geology, history, ecology, wildlife and other topics. There are also guided hikes, youth programs and evening talks at Zion Lodge and Watchman Campground. Current ranger programs are listed at visitor centers and posted on bulletin boards throughout the park.

Other Activities

TRAM TOUR

From April through October, a narrated tram tour departs from Zion Lodge and heads to the Temple of Sinawava. Lasting 60–75 minutes, the open-air tram lets you enjoy the beauty of Zion Canyon at a slower pace than the free shuttle. Tram tours depart Monday, Wednesday and Friday at 5:30pm. Tickets ($17 per person) are available at Zion Lodge.

HORSEBACK RIDES

From March through October, Canyon Trail Rides (canyonrides.com, 435-679-8665) offers guided horseback tours departing from the Court of the Patriarchs (p.146). There's a one-hour Virgin River ride ($45 per person), or a three-hour Sand Bench Ride ($90 per person), which explores Sentinel Slide (p.145).

Sunrise & Sunset in Zion

Zion's tall cliffs block the horizon in much of the park, but you can still enjoy the sun's first and last rays illuminating Zion's highest peaks. At sunrise and sunset, Zion's rocks radiate brilliant Southwestern colors. The back patio of the Human History Museum is a great place to watch sunrise light up the Towers of the Virgin (p.138). The Pa'rus Trail (p.134) is a great place to enjoy sunset. Canyon Junction (p.142) draws hordes of landscape photographers, who crowd the small bridge at sunset. Other great sunset lookouts include the short Archaeology Trail (p.133) or the longer Watchman Trail (p.172), which both start near the Zion Canyon Visitor Center. Another great sunset destination is Kolob Terrace (p.249), which has clear western views above Cave Valley and at Lava Point.

The Zion Forever Project

This wonderful nonprofit helps protect and preserve Zion National Park for future generations through a combination of fundraising, public programs, volunteer opportunities and much more. The Zion Forever Project operates all bookstores and gift shops in the park. It also offers a wide variety of events and experiences throughout the year, including field classes, guided hikes, lectures, and service projects. (zionpark.org, 435-772-3264)

Death in Zion

Zion's soaring cliffs and plunging canyons lure millions of visitors each year. But this beautiful landscape should never be taken for granted. Falls, flash floods and freak accidents have claimed dozens of lives over the past century, and 50–80 of search-and-rescue operations are conducted each year. As with any natural area, Zion comes with inherent risks. But there are some important things to keep in mind. Over three-quarters of deaths involve males, particularly young males in their teens and 20s—a group predisposed to risky behavior. And though accidents can happen to visitors of any age or gender, the number of deaths (dozens) is remarkably small compared to the total number of visitors (tens of millions). As long as you use common sense and exercise caution in risky areas, you should be fine. When in doubt, talk to a park ranger. To learn more about death in Zion—and more importantly how to prevent it—pick up a copy of *Death and Rescues in Zion* by Dave Nally.

Falling Deaths

Zion's most deadly hike, Angels Landing (p.174), includes a final push along a thin ridge with thousand-foot dropoffs on either side. Since the trail was constructed in 1926, it has claimed more than a dozen lives—but the vast majority of those fatalities occurred over the past two decades. Prior to 2000, just one person died on Angels Landing. Since then, a hiker has fallen roughly every two years on average. Another deadly trail in Zion is, oddly, one of the easiest: Emerald Pools, where three people have slipped from Middle Pool and fallen to their deaths. Lady Mountain, where two people died by 1967, was considered so dangerous it was ultimately shut down (p.154). Other trails with known fatalities include Observation Point (p.204), Hidden Canyon (p.208) and The Subway (p.256).

The Narrows

The Narrows (p.184) is one of Zion's most popular hikes, yet this magnificent slot canyon is prone to flash floods (p.16), particularly during monsoon season from July to September. The Narrows' first fatalities occurred on September 17, 1961, when five hikers were killed by a 15-foot wall of water roaring through the canyon at 15 miles per hour. Today park officials closely monitor the weather and prohibit access to The Narrows whenever flash floods are likely. Since 1961, there have been just three flash flood deaths in The Narrows.

In April 2010, two young men from Las Vegas built a raft out of logs and attempted to float through The Narrows while capturing their adventure on video. Their goal, according to reports, was to submit the video to a competition to appear on the reality TV show "Man Vs. Wild." Neither person was wearing a wetsuit or life jacket when they launched their homemade raft in the 40-degree Virgin River, which was flowing above 400 cubic feet per second. The raft broke apart in The Narrows, and both men drowned.

Rock Climbing

Modern rock climbing kicked off in Zion in 1967, when the park lifted a rock-climbing ban and began issuing permits for technical climbs on big walls. For nearly three decades not a single rock climbing death was reported. In 1997, the first rock climber died, and since then there have been roughly a half-dozen climbing deaths, all of which resulted from falls.

Canyoneering

Canyoneering (p.23) is one of Zion's most rewarding adventures, but it has claimed more lives (17) than any other activity in the park. Slot canyons are steep, rugged and prone to flash floods—in other words, they are inherently risky places. But as with rock climbing, proper training dramatically lowers the risks. Many canyoneering deaths result from falls, which often occur when people are fatigued and rushing through basic procedures. The deadliest tragedy in Zion's history occurred in Keyhole Canyon, the park's most popular beginner canyon, when a flash flood killed seven people on Sept. 14, 2015. Despite warnings that flash floods were probable, the group of novice canyoneers entered Keyhole Canyon around 4pm, shortly before a thunderstorm dropped a half-inch of rain on the canyon's drainage.

Lightning Strikes

Afternoon thunderstorms are common during monsoon season (p.35), and you should always avoid high, exposed areas whenever lightning is visible or thunder is audible. In 1908, lightning struck and killed two people on Cable Mountain (p.120), where a large metal cable-and-pulley system once acted like a giant lightning rod.

Zion Tunnel

Two people died during the construction of Zion Tunnel (p.220), and since 1986 the tunnel has experienced four fatalities, all of which involved motorcyclists colliding with tunnel walls.

West Temple, above Springdale

GATEWAY TOWNS

ZION WELCOMES OVER four million visitors a year, but the park is home to just one overnight lodge and three campgrounds. As a result, the majority of visitors stay in one of the small gateway towns just outside the park. There are dozens of private hotels and campgrounds near the park, and listing them here would take dozens of pages. Rather than waste all that paper—when all you need is one room or campsite—I've posted all lodging/camping information free on my website: jameskaiser.com

SOUTH ENTRANCE

Springdale

Located next to Zion's most popular entrance, Springdale is the biggest town near the park. Although its official year-round population is just over 500, there are scores of hotels, restaurants, gift shops and outfitters catering to visitors, making the town feel much larger. Most businesses are located along Zion Park Boulevard, which twists through the center of Springdale en route to Zion's South Entrance. Technically, Springdale is located *inside* Zion Canyon, with West Temple rising to the west, The Watchman rising to the east, and the Virgin River flowing through the center of the canyon. Many of the sandstone cliffs rising above town rival those in the park, adding an air of magnificence to Springdale.

Springdale Restaurants

★ KING'S LANDING $$$ (Dinner)
Springdale's top splurge. Charred octopus, charcuterie, cheese appetizers. Hearty entrees (steak, pork chops, king salmon) with sophisticated sides (peperonata, andouille sausage). Good wine list, full bar. (435-772-7422, 1515 Zion Park Blvd.)

★ THE SPOTTED DOG $$$ (Breakfast, Lunch, Dinner)
Tasty bistro with upscale entrees (wild game meatloaf, filet mignon, Muscovy duck), plus burgers and pasta. The breakfast buffet is one of the best deals in town. Good wine list, full bar. (435-772-0700, 450 Zion Park Blvd.)

★WHIPTAIL GRILL $$$ (Lunch, Dinner)

For satisfying Mexican (chipotle chicken enchiladas, mahi-mahi tacos, goat cheese chile relleno), plus juicy burgers and wings, head to this hip desert-retro grill, located in a former gas station. (435-772-0283, 445 Zion Park Blvd.)

★THAI SAPA $$$ (Lunch, Dinner)

Thai and Asian classics expertly prepared with high-quality ingredients. Delicious curries and noodle dishes. (435-772-0510, 198 Zion Park Blvd.)

MEME'S $$$ (Breakfast, Lunch, Dinner)

Casual restaurant famous for tasty burgers and crêpes (both sweet and savory), plus hearty sandwiches and breakfasts. (435-772-0114, 975 Zion Park Blvd.)

CAFÉ SOLEIL $$$ (Breakfast, Lunch, Dinner)

Charming hippie cafe with lots of delicious, healthy options: sandwiches, paninis, soups, baked goods, smoothies and coffee. (435-772-0505, 205 Zion Park Blvd.)

BIT & SPUR $$$ (Dinner)

Old West saloon with Mexican classics (carne asada, mole chicken, burritos), plus ribs, steak and pasta. Great margaritas. (435-772-3498, 1212 Zion Park Blvd.)

DEEP CREEK COFFEE $$$ (Breakfast, Lunch)

This rustic/hip cafe (open 6:30am) is a local favorite for top-notch coffee, tasty pastries and delicious breakfast sandwiches. (435-669-8849, 932 Zion Park Blvd.)

ZION BREWERY $$$ (Lunch, Dinner)

Located next to Zion's pedestrian entrance, this popular brewpub lures a steady stream of hungry visitors exiting the park. (435-772-0336, 95 Zion Park Blvd.)

Springdale Groceries

Sol Foods (435-772-3100, 995 Zion Park Blvd.) is Springdale's best grocery store, with a good selection of fruits, veggies, meats, packaged foods and healthy options. There's also the smaller Happy Camper Market (435-772-7805, 95 Zion Park Blvd.) near Zion's pedestrian entrance, a short walk from Watchman and South Campgrounds. Beer is available at both markets.

Wine & Liquor

Utah's strict liquor laws, which are heavily influenced by the state's Mormon culture, do not permit sales of wine, liquor or beer with alcohol content above 4% in supermarkets or convenience stores. A good selection of wine, liquor and strong beer is available at the Switchback Liquor Store (435-772-3700, 1149 Zion Park Blvd., closed Sundays and all holidays).

Springdale Outfitters

★ ZION ADVENTURE COMPANY

The largest outfitter in Springdale, ZAC got its start renting Narrows hiking gear, and its guides helped design the world's first canyoneering shoe. Today ZAC also offers guided hiking, canyoneering and rock climbing, plus bike rentals and much more. (36 Lion Blvd., 435-772-1001, zionadventures.com)

★ ZION GURU

Another great outfitter for Narrows hiking gear, guided Narrows hikes, plus canyoneering, rock climbing and all things yoga: outdoor yoga, yoga hikes, adventure yoga. (435-632-0432, zionguru.com)

ZION OUTFITTERS

Located right next to the park's pedestrian entrance, Zion Outfitters is a convenient place to rent Narrows hiking gear, bicycles or inner tubes to float the Virgin River (May–July). Hot showers also available. (435-772-5090, zionoutfitter.com)

ZION CYCLES

Full-service bike shop with half-day, full-day and multi-day bicycle rentals. From leisurely trips in Zion Canyon to adrenaline-fueled romps on mountain biking trails just outside the park, Zion Cycles has you covered. Guided trips also available. (435-772-0400, zioncycles.com)

ZION ROCK AND MOUNTAIN GUIDES

Zion's rock climbing specialists, with a full-service gear and rental shop, plus guided rock climbing and canyoneering classes. Overnight camping adventures also available. (435-772-3303, zionrockguides.com)

Rockville

Tiny, quaint Rockville (population 250) is located just three miles west of Springdale (a five-minute drive)—but it feels a world apart. While Springdale is filled with restaurants, gift shops and large hotels, Rockville is a mellow community on the banks of the Virgin River with a sprinkling of humble homes and a handful of charming bed-and-breakfasts.

Grafton

This ghost town (population 0), located just south of Rockville, was settled in 1859, abandoned in 1944, and used as the setting of the famous Paul Newman/Katherine Ross bicycle scene in 1969's "Butch Cassidy and the Sundance Kid." To visit the abandoned buildings, head south on Bridge Road in Rockville, cross the bridge over the Virgin River, and follow the signs to Grafton.

KOLOB TERRACE

Virgin

The small town of Virgin (population 600) is the start of Kolob Terrace Road, which rises 4,000 vertical feet through Zion's Kolob Terrace region (p.249). Virgin is home to a handful of hotels and campgrounds, and each October the town hosts the Red Bull Rampage, an extreme mountain biking competition.

Hurricane & La Verkin

Hurricane (pronounced *HUR-uh-kin* by locals) is the largest town (population 17,000) near Zion's South Entrance. First settled in 1896, it was named by a horse-drawn buggy driver, who, after experiencing a powerful gust of wind, exclaimed "Well, that was a hurricane. We'll name this Hurricane Hill." Today Hurricane's main street is lined with a combination of mom-and-pop shops, chain hotels and big box retailers. La Verkin (population 4,000) is located just north of Hurricane. Both towns are located a bit more than 20 miles (40-minute drive) from Zion's South Entrance.

★ ZION HELICOPTERS

Nothing puts Zion's rugged landscape in perspective like the view from the air. Although scenic helicopter flights are not allowed in Zion National Park, you can view much of the park along its boundary—or visit other gorgeous areas in southern Utah. (435-668-4185, zionhelicopters.com)

Restaurants

★ RIVER ROCK ROASTING $$$ (Breakfast, Lunch, Dinner)

Perched on a dramatic bluff overlooking the Virgin River gorge, this indie cafe draws devoted locals for its delicious coffee, smoothies and craft beer, plus sandwiches, salads and pizza. (435-635-7625, 394 South State St.)

★ STAGE COACH GRILLE $$$ (Breakfast, Lunch, Dinner)

The best restaurant in Hurricane/La Verkin, serving Western cuisine (steaks, pork chops, burgers), seafood and pasta in a lively, laid-back atmosphere. Local beers, plus wine and cocktails. (435-635-7400, 99 North State St.)

Wine & Liquor

The Utah State Liquor Store in Hurricane has a great selection of wine, liquor and strong craft beer. (435-627-8622, 202 Foothills Canyon Dr.)

St. George

With a population of 150,000, greater St. George is the largest city in Utah outside the Wasatch Front (which encompasses Salt Lake City). In 2018, St. George was the fastest-growing metropolitan city in the United States thanks to a steady influx of retirees and California migrants looking for affordable real estate, a balmy climate, and easy access to Utah's stunning natural beauty. St. George is located roughly 40 miles (a one-hour-drive) from Zion's South Entrance.

★THE DESERT RAT

The best outdoor specialty store in St. George, founded and staffed by local experts. (435-628-7277, 468 West St. George Blvd.)

ST. GEORGE DINOSAUR DISCOVERY SITE

Home to 200-million-year-old dinosaur tracks, which were discovered in 2000. Ancient fossils are also on display. (435-574-3466, 2180 East Riverside Dr.)

BRIGHAM YOUNG WINTER HOME

Early Mormon leader Brigham Young kept a winter home in St. George, and free tours are offered Monday–Saturday. (435-673-2517, 67 W 200 N)

JACOB HAMBLIN HOME

The 1863 home of famed Mormon explorer Jacob Hamblin (p.114) is a great place to learn about pioneer-era Utah. (435-673-5181, 3325 Santa Clara Dr.)

EAST ENTRANCE

Mt. Carmel Junction

Located 12 miles east of Zion's East Entrance, this tiny outpost (population 100) offers a handful of services (food, gas, lodging) at the intersection of Utah State Route 9 and Highway 89.

THUNDERBIRD $$$ (Breakfast, Lunch, Dinner)

This retro-diner has been family-owned since 1931. Burgers, sandwiches, wraps, salads and "Ho-Made Pies." (435-648-2262, Junction UT-9/Hwy. 89)

Kanab

The biggest little town east of Zion (population 4,500), Kanab has a wide range of services for travelers (gas, lodging, restaurants). Located 30 miles from Zion's East Entrance (a 40-minute-drive), Kanab also makes a great jumping-off point for day trips to Grand Staircase-Escalante National Monument.

GEOLOGY

To STAND ON the floor of Zion Canyon surrounded by 2,000-foot sandstone cliffs, face to face with a quarter billion years of history, is a humbling experience. Few landscapes offer such a compelling glimpse of earth's inner workings. If it weren't for an enormous chasm 60 miles south in Arizona, Zion would likely be the most famous canyon in America.

Anyone can marvel at the physical beauty of Zion. But take the time to learn about the extraordinary forces that sculpted the park—from the age of dinosaurs to the present—and Zion becomes transcendent. What was impressive becomes miraculous. What was beautiful becomes sublime.

The first people to gaze upon Zion used myths and legends to comprehend the landscape. Over the past century and a half, geologists have provided scientific explanations. And yet geology's revelations are often stranger, bolder, more unlikely, and more terrifying than any creation myth.

On a human timescale, Zion seems peaceful and serene. On a geologic timescale, it is young, violent and exciting. Earth is over four billion years old, but Zion Canyon formed in just two million years. Viewed against the full scope of geologic history, two million years is the blink of an eye. It's as if southern Utah suddenly cracked open and—*bam!*—there was Zion Canyon.

In reality, Zion was sliced open by the Virgin River, which tumbles down 9,000-foot mountains, flows 160 miles across an arid landscape, and empties into Lake Mead. During floods the Virgin picks up staggering amounts of sediment, turning it into a river of liquid sandpaper. Over millions of years the Virgin's floods cut through the landscape like a knife through a cake, sculpting fabulous canyons and exposing previously hidden layers of time.

Those exposed rock layers—nine in Zion alone—reveal ancient landscapes completely different from the scenery we enjoy today. Southern Utah was once home to tropical islands, steamy jungles, and vast sandy deserts. Many of these ancient landscapes lasted far longer than present-day Zion. But in our fortunate geologic moment, Zion showcases these long-buried volumes of earth history in chronological order. So step back, put on your geological spectacles, and discover how these prehistoric worlds came to be.

ANCIENT ROCKS

Earth's crust is composed of roughly a dozen interlocking tectonic plates that ride currents generated by molten rock below. Moving a few centimeters per year, tectonic plates constantly rearrange themselves. About 300 million years ago, Earth's plates smashed the continents together to form a supercontinent called Pangea. During this time North America lay near the equator, and Utah lay along the west coast. Just offshore, under a shallow tropical sea, lay Zion.

Over millions of years, shells and skeletons of dead sea creatures accumulated in thick layers on top of Zion. Eventually these layers cemented and compressed into Kaibab Limestone, which can be seen in present-day Kolob Canyons. Kaibab Limestone is one of the oldest rocks in Zion, but it's the youngest rock in Grand Canyon, forming the topmost layer capping both rims.

About 252 million years ago, roughly 90% of all species on earth died. This mass extinction—the largest in history—was triggered by massive volcanic eruptions in Siberia, which led to extreme ocean acidification and climate change. The great extinction marked the start of the Triassic Period, when surviving reptiles evolved into dinosaurs. During this time, the ocean retreated and advanced over Zion, depositing layers of sand, silt and mud. These layers ultimately compressed into sandstone, siltstone and shale that make up the Moenkopi Formation today.

As tectonic plates continued to shift, the coast migrated west and Zion found itself in a swampy, inland environment filled with ferns and conifers. Streams and lakes sheltered amphibians, freshwater clams and crocodile-like predators. Mammals appeared for the first time. Over millions of years, rivers and lakes deposited sediments that compacted into Chinle Formation rocks. A section of the Chinle Formation, called the Petrified Forest Member, is filled with ancient trees that were buried and mineralized, forming fossil logs. The Chinle Formation stretches across southern Utah into northern Arizona, where it forms the Painted Desert and Petrified Forest National Park.

PANGEA

About 210 million years ago, tectonic shifts placed North America in the hot, dry band of trade winds between 10 and 30 degrees latitude. During this time Utah became more arid. Streams and ponds continued to deposit sediment layers, however, and these layers compressed into siltstones, sandstones and shales known today as the Moenave Formation.

About 200 million years ago Pangea split down the middle. Europe and Africa drifted east, and enormous quantities of magma and noxious gases poured forth

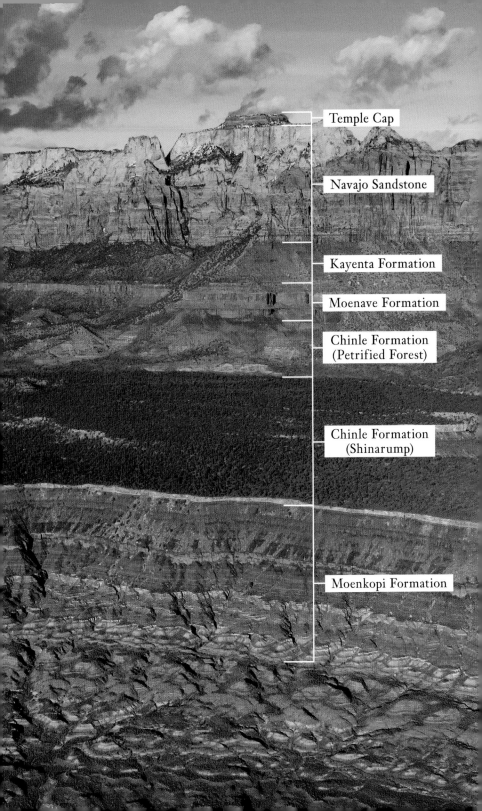

Temple Cap

Navajo Sandstone

Kayenta Formation

Moenave Formation

Chinle Formation
(Petrified Forest)

Chinle Formation
(Shinarump)

Moenkopi Formation

Kayenta Formation waterfalls

from the seams. This led to runaway global warming, triggering another mass extinction that killed over 30% of all species. In the wake of the die-off, dinosaurs reigned supreme, ushering in a new period called the Jurassic.

During the early Jurassic, southwest Utah had a lake and river system that flowed across a broad coastal plain. Dry winters followed rainy summers, and rivers flowing from the east deposited over 500 feet of sediment that compressed into dark red siltstones and sandstones known today as Kayenta Formation. Three-toed dinosaurs called theropods walked across the muddy landscape, and their tracks are sometimes preserved in Kayenta-era rocks.

As tectonic plates shifted, mountains rose in Nevada and California, sucking moisture out of western winds and sending dry air across Utah. By about 190 million years ago, Utah was home to the largest sand dune desert that ever existed on earth, covering nearly 150,000 square miles. In Zion the sand gathered to a depth of 2,200 feet, topped by sand dunes 150 feet tall.

Where did all the sand come from? The answer lies in the early formation of Pangea. When Europe smashed into North America it pushed up the ancient Appalachian Mountains, which once rivaled the Himalayas in size. As the Appalachians eroded over tens of millions of years, rivers carried away the debris. One river—which may have been as large as the Amazon—stretched as far as Wyoming, depositing Appalachian debris that blew south over Utah. For over 40 million years, giant sand dunes covered the Four Corners region.

Around 160 million years ago global sea levels rose, and the Sundance Sea, which connected to the Arctic Ocean, washed across the sand dunes from the

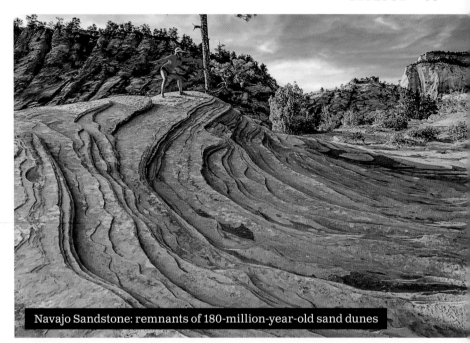
Navajo Sandstone: remnants of 180-million-year-old sand dunes

north. As minerals from the Sundance Sea seeped through the sand they "glued" the grains together into Navajo Sandstone. (The name comes from Navajo lands in northern Arizona where the rock was first identified.) Today exposed Navajo Sandstone reveals diagonal "cross-beds" created by the faces of ancient sand dunes. By studying cross-bed angles, geologists can determine which direction the wind blew when the dunes formed. Although dinosaurs flourished throughout this period, Navajo Sandstone contains very few fossils because thirsty dinosaurs avoided the dry dunes.

When Zion lay along the shore of the Sundance Sea, tidal flats composed of red mud covered the landscape, eventually compressing into mudstone. As sea levels varied, sandstone and limestone also formed, and together these layers make up the Temple Cap Formation—named because it caps Zion's sandstone rock formations, which early geologists called "temples."

As the Sundance Sea expanded, it stretched across Utah into Arizona and Nevada. This period marked the formation of Zion's youngest rock layer, the Carmel Formation, which is composed of limestone and filled with marine fossils including clams, oysters, and crinoids.

The next major period, the Cretaceous, started 145 million years ago and ended 80 million years later when an asteroid smashed into Earth, ending the age of dinosaurs. Throughout much of the Cretaceous additional rock layers formed on top of Zion, burying older rocks deep underground. How those older rocks ultimately ended up thousands of feet *above* sea level is the next chapter in the geologic story.

COLORADO PLATEAU

Geographers divide the United States into roughly two dozen provinces, and the Colorado Plateau, which covers 130,000 square miles in the Four Corners region, is one of them. Geologically, the Colorado Plateau is notable for its stability. While the Rocky Mountains twisted and contorted land to the east, and the Basin and Range province stretched and pulled land to the west, the Colorado Plateau's colorful sedimentary layers remained gloriously intact.

In fact, the Colorado Plateau has not experienced serious deformation in over half a billion years. This is particularly remarkable given its size—the Colorado Plateau is the second-largest plateau in the world after the Tibetan Plateau—and the powerful forces that have acted on it from below.

About 80 million years ago, the last sea covering Utah retreated and deep forces began pushing up the Colorado Plateau. The exact mechanisms of this uplift remain a mystery. What is known is that the rise has not been constant. Uplift started off slow, and then, from 25 million to 5 million years ago, the plateau rose nearly 130 feet every million years. Over the past 5 million years, uplift accelerated to 730 feet every million years—a nearly fivefold increase.

The Colorado Plateau now rests over a mile above sea level, yet its sedimentary rock layers remain as neatly defined as a wedding cake. Some geologists think the Colorado Plateau resisted deformation because earth's crust is relatively thick in the Four Corners region—up to 25 miles deep in places. The crust of the nearby Great Basin Desert, by contrast, is just 16 miles deep. So rather than buckle and break as it rose, the Colorado Plateau remained relatively unaltered as a single tectonic block.

Of course, the rise of the Colorado Plateau has not been entirely smooth. The uplift created dozens of giant faults (cracks), especially along its boundaries. The southwestern edge of the Colorado Plateau rose particularly high, tilting slightly

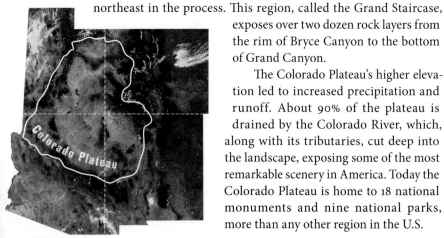

northeast in the process. This region, called the Grand Staircase, exposes over two dozen rock layers from the rim of Bryce Canyon to the bottom of Grand Canyon.

The Colorado Plateau's higher elevation led to increased precipitation and runoff. About 90% of the plateau is drained by the Colorado River, which, along with its tributaries, cut deep into the landscape, exposing some of the most remarkable scenery in America. Today the Colorado Plateau is home to 18 national monuments and nine national parks, more than any other region in the U.S.

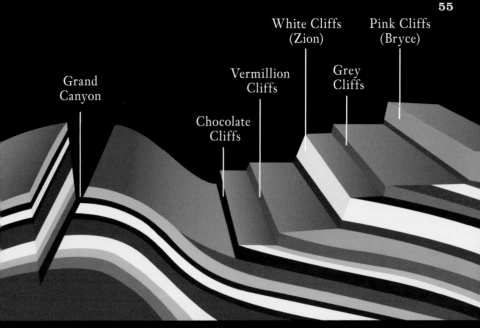

White Cliffs
(Zion)

Pink Cliffs
(Bryce)

Grand
Canyon

Vermillion
Cliffs

Grey
Cliffs

Chocolate
Cliffs

The Grand Staircase

From the rim of Bryce Canyon, perched 9,000 feet above sea level, nearly two billion years of exquisite rock layers cascade down to the bottom of Grand Canyon in stairstep fashion. This remarkable showcase, first noted by geologist Clarence Dutton (p.64), reveals more geologic history than any place on earth, making it one of the highlights of the Colorado Plateau.

Over millions of years, as the Colorado Plateau uplifted, its southwest edge broke along faults and tilted northeast, revealing nearly two dozen rock layers in just over 100 miles. Five major steps make up the 200-mile-wide Grand Staircase. The youngest, topmost step, just 45 million years old, is formed by the Pink Cliffs in Bryce Canyon and Cedar Breaks. Below the Pink Cliffs lie the Gray Cliffs, which consist of sandstone and shale. Below the Gray Cliffs are the White Cliffs of Zion National Park, named for light-colored Navajo Sandstone. The Vermillion Cliffs, tinted brilliant hues thanks to iron oxide and manganese, lie below Zion, followed by the Chocolate Cliffs colored brown by mudstone. At that point a bulge in the landscape pushes the remaining rock layers up to the North Rim of Grand Canyon. From there a dozen rock formations tumble 6,000 vertical feet to the Colorado River, which slices through 1.8-billion-year-old Vishnu Schist, the oldest exposed rock on the Colorado Plateau.

The rock layers of the Grand Staircase reveal over two dozen prehistoric landscapes—from the time before vertebrates to the rise and fall of the dinosaurs. Traveling through this mesmerizing landscape is like stepping into a real-life time machine.

THE DIRTY VIRGIN

At first glance, the Virgin River doesn't seem impressive. For most of the year it flows cool and clear through Zion Canyon, averaging just 100 cubic feet per second (cfs)—less than one percent of the Colorado River's flow in Grand Canyon. But the Virgin River is coy and deceptive. Over the past two million years, during fits of rage, it has sculpted one of the world's most dramatic canyons.

The Virgin River originates near Navajo Lake on Cedar Mountain, just south of Cedar Breaks National Monument. From its 9,000-foot headwaters, the North Fork of the Virgin River tumbles towards Zion, flowing through the Narrows and emerging into Zion Canyon. Another branch of the Virgin, the East Fork, flows through Parunuweap Canyon and connects with the North Fork just south of Zion National Park.

From the confluence of the North Fork and East Fork, the Virgin flows south across the Utah border into Arizona and Nevada, ultimately emptying into Lake Mead. In just 160 miles the Virgin River falls 7,800 feet—roughly 50 feet per mile. In Zion Canyon, its gradient is even greater: 71 feet per mile—nearly ten times steeper than the Colorado River in Grand Canyon.

This steep gradient is what gives the Virgin River its superpower. A fast river carries more sediment than a slow river, leading to more erosion. Although the Virgin averages just 100 cfs throughout the year, during floods it can top 9,000 cfs—90 times greater than normal flow. More sediment in the river leads to more erosion, which adds more sediment in a self-reinforcing cycle. A river flowing ten times faster carries 2,000 times more sediment. The Virgin River at 9,000 cfs carries nearly three million times more sediment than average flows. A single flood can remove more dirt in a day than a normal flow removes all year.

During floods the sediment-heavy Virgin grinds down the landscape. High flows tumble rocks and boulders like ice cubes, gouging the streambed bit by bit. Each year the Virgin River carries roughly one million tons of sediment through Zion Canyon—an average of 366 dump trucks of dirt *each day*—cutting downward at a rate of roughly 1.3 feet every 1,000 years. In the depths of the Ice Age, when increased precipitation produced bigger floods, the rate of cutting was even higher. Over the past two million years, Virgin River floods have sliced through over 2,000 feet of Navajo Sandstone in Zion.

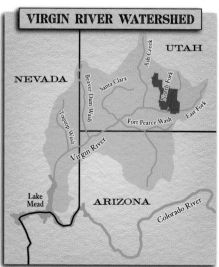

VIRGIN RIVER WATERSHED

Ash Creek

UTAH

NEVADA

Beaver Dam Wash

Santa Clara

North Fork

East Fork

Fort Pearce Wash

Toroweap Wash

Virgin River

Lake Mead

ARIZONA

Colorado River

THE CANYON WIDENS

The Virgin River is incredibly effective at cutting down vertically—but not so effective at cutting horizontally. This is most evident in The Narrows, which is a thousand feet deep and less than 20 feet wide in places. And yet 25 miles downstream the mouth of Zion Canyon is over a mile wide.

Canyon widening is largely determined by Zion's rock layers. The Narrows is carved entirely out of Navajo Sandstone, which is relatively strong and forms steep cliffs. But just below Navajo Sandstone lies the relatively soft Kayenta Formation. When the Virgin River comes into contact with the Kayenta Formation it erodes the soft rock much faster than Navajo Sandstone. Left unsupported from below, chunks of Navajo Sandstone collapse and tumble into the Virgin River, where they eventually wash away during floods. As this process repeats itself, the canyon grows wider. Not surprisingly, the downstream entrance to the Narrows is exactly the point where the Virgin River reaches the lower limit of Navajo Sandstone and flows over Kayenta Formation.

Farther downstream, however, the Virgin River flows through the center of a wide canyon, never touching the canyon walls. What accounts for canyon widening there? Navajo Sandstone, it turns out, is an excellent aquifer. Rain and melted snow slowly trickles down through the porous sandstone, and when this water reaches the bottom of Navajo Sandstone it comes into contact with Kayenta Formation. Although Kayenta Formation is softer than Navajo Sandstone, it's less porous and thus acts as a barrier to water. Prevented from flowing down, water flows sideways and emerges from Navajo Sandstone as seeps and springs. Water flowing from these seeps and springs slowly erodes the exposed Kayenta Formation, undercutting the Navajo Sandstone once again.

More conventional forms of erosion also chip away at Zion. One of the most destructive is frost wedging, which happens when water freezes and expands in the cracks of rocks. This produces massive pressures—up to 20,000 pounds per square inch—capable of spliting rocks apart. Frost wedging sometimes triggers massive rockfalls that send giant chucks of sandstone crashing down.

Side canyons also contribute to erosion, but their small, intermittent streams can't always keep up with the Virgin River's fast rate of downward cutting. Over time, many of these side canyons end up as "hanging valleys" perched high above the floor of Zion Canyon, forming spectacular waterfalls when it rains.

When the Virgin River reaches the town of Springdale it cuts through the Chinle Formation—the softest rock in Zion. At this point the canyon grows even wider, yawning open until it's no longer considered a canyon. But the Virgin River's work is hardly over. Erosion is an ongoing process, and there are still plenty of rocks left to cut through upstream. In the future, erosion will transform the current Narrows into a wide canyon like Springdale—and a new Narrows will form many miles upstream.

RECENT CATASTROPHES

Over the past five million years, the Colorado Plateau uplifted five times faster than it did in the previous 20 million years. Geologists still don't know why, but one theory involves an enormous chunk of earth's hard upper mantle, which lies directly below the crust, dislodging from the Colorado Plateau and dropping into the hot lower mantle below. This may have made the Colorado Plateau more buoyant, particularly if hot, viscous material from the lower mantle flowed into the gap.

The rapid uplift formed cracks in the Colorado Plateau's western boundary, and lava sometimes poured out. Over the past 1.4 million years at least six lava flows have covered portions of Zion. The most recent flow, which took place 100,000 years ago at Crater Hill (p.243), sent lava tumbling into the Virgin River near the present-day ghost town of Grafton. The resulting dam created a ten-square-mile lake that stretched to the current visitor center.

Another lake formed 4,800 years ago when the Sentinel Slide (p.145) sent ten billion cubic feet of rock tumbling into the Virgin River. The rock dam formed 400-foot-deep Lake Sentinel, which stretched five miles upstream to the Temple of Sinawava. Before Lake Sentinel, Zion was a steep V-shaped canyon. But as hundreds of feet of lake sediments accumulated, the bottom of the lake flattened out. When the Virgin River broke through the dam seven centuries later, the lake drained and upper Zion Canyon found itself with a beautiful flat floor.

Powerful geological forces continue to shape the region. In 1992, a 5.9 magnitude earthquake struck near St. George, Utah. In Zion, 30 miles distant, it triggered a landslide 3,600 feet wide that blocked the park's South Entrance. The earthquake was likely due to movement along the Hurricane Fault, a 155-mile active fault just west of Zion that might someday produce bigger earthquakes.

In 2001, a Rockville man awoke at 5:35 a.m. when a 250-ton boulder crashed into his bathroom. His bedroom roof collapsed within one foot of his bed, and a second 500-ton boulder landed in his front yard. There had been no earthquakes or heavy rains; the giant boulders simply broke away from the cliffs above.

And yet rain and water are still the most important forces shaping Zion today. In 1995, heavy rains triggered a landslide that destroyed a portion of Zion Canyon Road. In 2018 a July rainstorm dumped three inches of rain in three hours, swelling the Virgin River to 5,410 cfs (its seventh-highest recorded flow) and triggering rockfalls that closed four popular trails.

As long as there's nature, there will be natural disasters. But it's worth remembering that these so-called catastrophes are responsible for the breathtaking scenery we enjoy today. Without earthquakes, rockfalls, volcanoes and floods, Zion would be just another flat, boring landscape. So consider yourself lucky. You're alive during that brief moment—geologically speaking—when you can enjoy one of nature's finest creations.

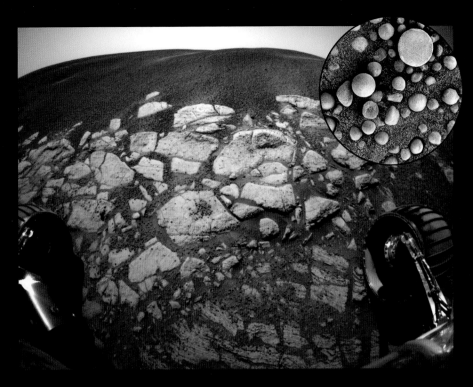

Zion on Mars

In 2004, NASA's Opportunity rover landed on Mars after a six-month journey. Its mission: find evidence of ancient water on Mars. A few sols (Martian days) after landing, Opportunity detected dozens of strange, round pebbles scattered across the ground near the landing site. NASA scientists called them "Martian blueberries," but Southwest geologists thought they looked remarkably similar to small, dark balls sometimes found on top of Navajo Sandstone. In Zion and other parks these balls are colloquially called Moqui marbles. (*Moqui* is a Hopi word that means "dear departed ones," and the Hopi believe spirits of the dead play marbles with these round rocks at night.) Moqui Marbles are made of sandstone and hematite (iron), but how exactly they form is a mystery. It's thought that when iron-rich water flows through Navajo Sandstone, hematite precipitates out and covers sand grains. These tiny spheres grow layer by layer, and some pieces clump together to form larger balls. After Opportunity detected hematite in the rocks, NASA scientists concluded that Martian blueberries provide evidence of a watery environment on ancient Mars. But that may be just the beginning. Some geologists speculate that Moqui Marbles form with the help of microbes. If true, Martian blueberries might offer evidence that life once existed on Mars.

Desert Varnish

This shiny dark coating, which varies in color from reddish-brown to black, covers many of the rocks and cliffs in Zion. Often just one micrometer thick, desert varnish is a combination of clay, iron, manganese and organic matter, but scientists are divided on how it forms. Some believe desert varnish is organic in nature, created by microorganisms on the rocks. Others think desert varnish is inorganic, the result of dissolved chemicals washing over the rock and leaving behind a thin coating. In some places desert varnish is thousands of years old. Black desert varnish is high in manganese; red desert varnish is high in iron. Throughout the Southwest, ancient humans were fond of scraping away the dark varnish to make petroglyphs.

Clarence Dutton

Many geologists have written about Zion, but few have done so as eloquently as Clarence Dutton. His early descriptions of the Colorado Plateau sparked national interest in the region, and his lyrical writing metamorphosized geological investigation into art.

As a young boy in Wallingford, Connecticut, Dutton was a voracious reader with a passion for rocks and minerals. He entered Yale at 15, fought in the Civil War, and achieved the rank of first lieutenant. In 1874 he was 33 and living in Washington, D.C.—"a lover of the good life, of cigars, drink, and society"—when his quick mind caught the attention of famed explorer John Wesley Powell. The one-armed Powell, who led the first Colorado River expedition through Grand Canyon in 1869, recruited Dutton to explore and map the region Powell called the Colorado Plateau. The stark geography—unlike anything on the East Coast—captivated Dutton. "There is an eloquence in forms," he wrote of Zion, "which stirs the imagination with a singular power and kindles in the mind a glowing response."

In 1880 Dutton published *Report on the Geology of the High Plateaus of Utah*, but his masterpiece is 1882's *Tertiary History of the Grand Cañon District*, a richly illustrated book that includes a description of "The Valley of the Virgin" (Zion). "Nothing can exceed the wondrous beauty of Little Zion Valley," Dutton wrote. "In its proportions it is about equal to Yo Semite, but in the nobility and beauty of the sculptures there is no comparison." Dutton's emotional prose contrasted with William Henry Holmes' hyperrealistic illustrations—a bold departure from the dull scientific descriptions and overly dramatic paintings that previously depicted the region.

After exploring the Southwest, Dutton studied volcanoes in Hawaii, made the first depth measurements of Crater Lake in Oregon, and became a founding member of the National Geographic Society. But his pioneering work on the Colorado Plateau, one of the planet's richest geological treasures, remains his greatest legacy.

"Temples and Towers of the Virgin," illustration by William Henry Holmes for Clarence Dutton's book *Tertiary History of the Grand Cañon District*.

ECOLOGY

AT FIRST GLANCE, Zion's sandstone cliffs and slickrock canyons seem barren and inhospitable. The rugged geography, combined with southern Utah's arid climate, suggests an impoverished biology. But in reality, the park is teeming with life. Zion covers less than 0.2 percent of the Colorado Plateau, yet it contains over 1,000 native plant species—nearly 60% of the region's plant species, the richest diversity in Utah. These plants form the base of a thriving food chain that supports over 400 vertebrate species, from delicate tree frogs to 250-pound mountain lions.

Zion's rich biodiversity results from several factors. With elevations ranging from 3,700 to 8,700 feet, the park encompasses a wide range of habitats. Sunbaked deserts are found at the lowest elevations. Cool alpine forests cover mountaintops blanketed in winter snow. Zion is also located at the intersection of three major geographic regions: the Colorado Plateau, the Mojave Desert and the Great Basin Desert. Plants and animals from each region find their way into the park, boosting the total number of species.

More than anything, however, life in Zion is determined by water. The stone canyons that slice through the park trace the phantom routes of prehistoric floods. Millennia upon millennia of runoff have washed away the negative space—and water continues to sculpt the landscape. Precipitation may not be consistent or regular, but it flows through the same predictable channels, offering a familiar lifeline in the otherwise parched terrain.

Zion's most important water source is the Virgin River. From its headwaters near Cedar Breaks National Monument, the Virgin tumbles down pine-covered slopes, flows through The Narrows, and twists through Zion Canyon. Melting snow swells the river in spring. Summer thunderstorms trigger flash floods. But for most of the year the Virgin flows soft and gentle, offering the desert's most prized commodity: dependable year-round water. The Virgin River shelters four native fish species, all of which evolved strong muscles and a keen sense of hydrodynamics to survive powerful floods.

The banks of the Virgin River in Zion Canyon are lined with vegetation. Looking down from the rim, it's easy to spot the green strip of plants tracing the river's curves. Cottonwood trees are the most obvious species, growing 60 feet or taller with a crown of heart-shaped leaves. Other deciduous trees include box elder, velvet ash and willows. Below the trees, water-loving plants like cattails and rushes grow alongside the river.

Outside of Zion Canyon there are 76 miles of perennial streams in the park. The well-watered habitat near rivers and streams is called the riparian zone. It's one of Zion's smallest habitats in terms of area—but one of the most important in terms of life. The riparian zone's thick vegetation provides habitat for dozens of animals, from birds to small mammals, which enjoy easy access to drinking water. Mosquitoes, wasps and other insects also thrive in the riparian zone, providing an all-you-can-eat buffet for bats after the sun goes down.

Set back from the rivers are a completely different group of plants and shrubs. Although just a stone's throw from dependable water, their world bears little resemblance to the lush riparian zone. These hardy plants live in dry soils that receive little rain. A lack of water defines their lives, and they have evolved some remarkable adaptations to cope with the harsh conditions. Thick, waxy coatings on some leaves and petals help retain water and reflect sunlight. Fourwing saltbush grows in soil too salty for other plants, excreting excess salt through tiny hairs and forming crystals that reflect sunlight.

Move even farther back from the river and, paradoxically, you'll find water again. The steep walls of Zion Canyon contain dozens of seeps and springs that nourish lush hanging gardens (p.72). This dependable water, fed by sandstone aquifers, emerges at the intersection of two important rock layers: Navajo Sandstone and Kayenta Formation (p.52). These springs are biological oases that are home to dozens of species. At similar sites in Grand Canyon, the number of species found at springs is *500 times* greater than in the surrounding desert.

High above the springs, on well-protected rock ledges, peregrine falcons and canyon wrens build nests, lay eggs and raise their young. Plants also grow on the cliffs, but their habitat is largely defined by the orientation of canyon walls. Cliffs cloaked in deep shadows support plants normally found at higher, cooler elevations. Cliffs bathed in sunlight support desert plants normally found at lower, hotter elevations. In some parts of Zion Canyon you can find Douglas fir, an alpine tree normally found thousands of feet higher, growing in cool, shaded areas just a few yards from sun-loving cacti.

The rim of Zion Canyon and the talus slopes directly below the cliffs are dotted with scraggly piñon pines and juniper (p.76). Found between 4,000 and 6,800 feet, piñon-juniper woodlands cover nearly half of Zion, making it the largest habitat in the park. Both trees are well-adapted to arid environments. Piñon pine nuts were a vital food for native tribes, and they are a staple of the piñon jay's diet. Mule deer and bighorn sheep browse shrubs in the piñon-juniper understory, hoping to avoid mountain lions that also call the woodlands home.

Hanging Garden

Set farther back from the canyon rims are forests of ponderosa pine, Zion's tallest tree. On high plateaus above 5,500 feet, annual precipitation can average 26 inches or more, enough to sustain the fast-growing trees, which cover more than 25,000 acres (about 16 percent of the park). Navajo Sandstone, which is porous and retains more water than other rocks, allows ponderosa pines in Zion to grow at lower than normal elevations.

The park's highest elevations are covered in mixed forests of Douglas fir, white pine and quaking aspen—scenery more like the Rockies than the desert Southwest. These alpine trees require cool temperatures and abundant precipitation, much of which arrives as winter snow. Black bears, marmot and pika gorge on luxuriant summer vegetation, hoping to gain enough weight to survive winter hibernation. Elk, the largest animals in Zion, do not hibernate, and during the cold winter months they nibble on tree bark and huddle together for warmth.

Spring snowmelt flows into slickrock canyons, providing the only reliable source of water during periods of drought. Slickrock is one of Zion's most inhospitable habitats—and yet hardy plants and animals still manage to call the exposed rocks home. A flower called Eastwood's paintbrush sends deep roots into rock crevices to find hidden pockets of water. Exposed water pockets, called potholes, nourish amphibians and tiny crustaceans. When evaporation robs potholes of water, some crustaceans dehydrate completely, entering periods of dormancy that can last decades. When water eventually returns, the crustaceans rehydrate and spring back to life.

HUMAN CHANGES

When Mormon settlers arrived in southern Utah in the mid-1800s, they encountered a harsh, rocky landscape. Through hard work and communal sacrifice they transformed the desert, building dams and irrigation channels that enabled large-scale farming and ranching. By 1900 there were roughly 15,000 sheep and 7,000 cattle in Washington County. But livestock overgrazing, combined with heavy logging in the ponderosa forests above Zion Canyon, affected local watersheds. With less vegetation to absorb summer thunderstorms, floods became more frequent and powerful.

Livestock also transmitted previously unknown diseases to native species. Desert bighorn sheep once flourished in southern Utah, but disease from domestic sheep decimated bighorn populations. By 1950 Zion's desert bighorn population, which once numbered in the hundreds, fell to zero. This followed the extirpation of the gray wolf, which local ranchers hunted out of the region over a decade earlier.

Invasive plants also took their toll. Cheatgrass, a European native covered in sharp barbs, first appeared on the U.S. East Coast in the 1860s. By the 1930s cheatgrass had spread across America, becoming the dominant grass in Zion Canyon. Another invasive plant, tamarisk, arrived from Eurasia in the late 1800s and spread along the banks of the Colorado River. Within a few decades much of the Colorado River and its tributaries, including the Virgin River, were overrun by tamarisk, which crowds out native plants.

Before white settlers arrived, natural fires were common in Zion's ponderosa forests. The low-intensity fires burned grasses and shrubs but left mature trees unharmed. Small fires also recyled nutrients and allowed new plants to grow. But in 1925, six years after Zion was declared a national park, fire suppression became official government policy because forest fires were viewed as threats. Over the following decades, fire suppression enabled the growth of dense forest understories, which fueled high-intensity fires capable of killing mature trees. As fires grew larger and more catastrophic, forest managers realized they had made a mistake. Park policy shifted, and periodic controlled burns were introduced to reduce fire hazards and return forests to a more natural state.

Other policies have been far more successful. The elimination of grazing and logging in Zion allowed vegetation to regrow in much of the Virgin River watershed, and eradication programs reduced tamarisk along riverbanks. Perhaps most significant, the Virgin River continued to flow freely—a sharp contrast to dozens of Western rivers plugged by dams in the 20th century. In 2009, federal legislation designated 144 river miles in Zion "Wild and Scenic," the first such designation in Utah. Today 90% of Zion is managed as wilderness, protecting dozens of sensitive species—including desert bighorn sheep, which were successfully reintroduced to the park in 1978.

Hanging Gardens

Cardinal Monkeyflower

Western Columbine

Zion Shooting Star

Some of Zion's most beautiful plants are found in hanging gardens, one of the desert's most fascinating habitats. Hanging gardens in Zion often form where water flows out of Navajo Sandstone near its contact point with the Kayenta rock formation below (p.52). Zion's year-round oases nourish water-loving plants that would otherwise perish in the desert. Among the star attractions are columbine: bell-shaped flowers that taper to five narrow tubes. Western columbine (*Aquilegia formosa*) are red and yellow, while golden columbine (*Aquilegia chrysantha*) bloom for much of the summer in hanging gardens. The Zion shooting star (*Dodecatheon pulchellum*) looks like a comet, with a sharp point trailed by yellow and lavender flowers. The bright red petals of cardinal monkeyflower (*Erythranthe cardinalis*) attract hummingbirds, whose foreheads touch the stamen, gathering pollen that's spread from flower to flower.

Yucca

One of the signature plants of the desert Southwest, yucca are easily identified by sharp, dagger-like leaves that grow up to two feet long. In spring a tall stalk filled with creamy white flowers rises from the center of the plant. Although sometimes misidentified as cacti, yucca are actually giant members of the lily family. Well-adapted to arid environments, curved leaves help yucca channel rainwater and dew towards their roots. Yucca were among the most useful and important plants for native tribes throughout the Southwest. In Zion the Southern Paiute wove the plant's strong fibers into ropes, baskets, mats and sandals (p.107). Yucca fruit was eaten, and yucca root was diced and put in water to make soap—a technique early Mormon settlers adopted from the Southern Paiute. There are three common yucca species in Zion: banana yucca (*Yucca baccata*), named for its banana-shaped fruit, Utah yucca (*Yucca utahensis*), which can grow up to ten feet tall, and the narrow-leaved yucca (*Yucca angustissima*), which has an unbranched flowering stalk.

Sacred Datura
Datura wrightii

These dazzling white flowers grow on sandy roadsides throughout the Southwest. In Zion they're so common some locals call them "Zion lilies." The petals, which can grow up to eight inches long, close into a tight cylinder on hot, sunny days to reduce evaporation and conserve water. When temperatures drop around dusk, the petals unfurl into the largest flower in Utah. Hawk moths with proboscis (tongues) up to a foot long drink datura nectar and pollinate the trumpet-shaped flowers at night. Sacred datura often bloom in spring, but flowers can appear any time of year with sufficient rain. The flower emits a foul odor, and all parts of the plant are toxic. But sacred datura is central to the religious ceremonies of indigenous tribes. The plant contains high doses of hallucinogenic alkaloids that shaman use to induce visions. Datura ceremonies frequently focus on rites of passage, and the visions people experience help determine their future roles within the tribe. Even low doses can be fatal, however, so unless you're an indigenous shaman don't try it.

Prickly Pear Cactus

Zion is home to four species of prickly pear cactus, all of which are easily identified by flat, green pads covered in spines. Vivid flowers, ranging from bright yellow to magenta, bloom in May and June. Native tribes harvested prickly pear fruit ("tuna") and the fleshy pads ("nopal"), both of which are still eaten in Mexico today. Some prickly pear pads are covered in white lumps. These are cochineal insects, which attach to prickly pear cacti, drink its liquid, and cover themselves in a sticky white substance for protection. When the bugs are crushed, they produce a luxurious scarlet color rarely found in nature. Aztec rulers cherished clothes stained red with cochineal, and following the conquest of Mexico dried cochineal became Spain's second-most valuable export after silver. The red dye colored everything from British military uniforms to American flags. Cochineal is still used today as a natural red dye in foods and cosmetics under the names "carmine" or "natural red 4."

Zion Wildflowers

Wildflowers bloom from March to October in Zion. Most flowers bloom in spring, but some species bloom in summer and fall. Delicate and ephemeral, wildflowers appear only for a short time following adequate precipitation. The seeds of many species are covered in a resinous coating that can only be removed by ample rain or melting snow. The coating acts as a natural auto-timer, triggering germination when sufficient water becomes available.

Desert Paintbrush
Castilleja chromosa

Gooseberry-leaf Globemallow
Sphaeralcea grossulariifolia

Eaton's Penstemon
Penstemon eatonii

Palmer's Penstemon
Penstemon palmeri

Purple Torch
Echinocereus engelmannii

Sego Lily
Calochortus nuttallii

Prince's Plume
Stanleya pinnata

Zion Shooting-star
Dodecatheon pulchellum

Showy Four-o'clock
Mirabilis multiflora

Western Columbine
Aquilegia formosaa

Tansyleaf Aster
Machaeranthera tanacetifolia

Prickly Pear
Opuntia

Cardinal Monkeyflower
Mimulus cardinalis

Silverleaf Nightshade
Solanum elaeagnifolium

Piñon-Juniper Woodlands

Piñon pines and junipers are two of the most common trees in the West, covering 100 million acres from Oregon to northern Mexico, including nearly half of Zion National Park. Piñon-juniper woodlands grow at elevations between 4,000 and 6,800 feet in Zion. An abundance of porous Navajo Sandstone, which retains more water than other rocks, allows piñon-juniper woodlands to grow at lower elevations in Zion than in other parts of Utah.

Utah Juniper
Juniperus osteosperma

Juniper trees are easily identified by their stringy bark, scaly green shoots, and tiny blue "berries." Distillers use juniper berries (which are actually tiny modified pine cones) to give gin its herbal flavor. The word "juniper" is actually derived from *genever,* the Dutch word for gin. Berries used in gin-making traditionally come from the common juniper, not the Utah juniper found in Zion. Growing up to 30 feet tall, Utah junipers send out deep roots in search of water. Tap roots can penetrate 25 feet, while lateral roots spread out 100 feet or more. This impressive root system accounts for up to two-thirds of the tree's total mass, allowing some junipers to grow even after they have been toppled over by the wind. Under optimal conditions junipers can live 500 years or more. Though not nearly as important as piñon pines to native tribes, juniper trees had many important uses. Women fashioned the soft, stringy bark into clothing. Juniper pollen was used ceremonially. And because juniper wood burns evenly with a steady flame, it was considered one of the best fuels for cooking fires.

Piñon Pine

Piñon pines are one of the most important food sources on the Colorado Plateau. Native tribes, modern foragers and wild animals all enjoy piñon pine nuts, which are nutritious, delicious and can be harvested in enormous quantities. There are two species of piñon pine in Zion: Colorado piñons (*Pinus edulis*), which have two needles, and singleleaf piñons (*Pinus monophylla*), the only pine tree in the world with just one needle. Both evolved from Mexican pines around 20 million years ago. As piñon pines spread north, their nuts became a favorite food of piñon jays, which gathered nuts by the thousands and buried them for later use. Leftover or forgotten nuts grew into new trees, and over millions of years piñons evolved new characteristics based on the kinds of nuts preferred by the birds. Most pine trees produce small nuts with "wings" so the wind can disperse the seeds. Piñon nuts, by contrast, became large and "wingless," and piñon pines are now completely dependent on piñon jays and other animals to spread their seeds far from the tree. When humans arrived in the Southwest, they quickly recognized the importance of piñon pines. In late summer, when piñon nuts ripen, native tribes harvested and stored as many nuts as possible. Piñon pines can grow 50 feet or taller, and pine cones on the highest branches were knocked down with long poles. Pine nuts were removed from the cones and then roasted, boiled or ground into flour on stone metates. During harsh winters, an adequate supply of pine nuts sometimes meant the difference between life and death. Pine nuts were central to native diets, and roughly 85 percent of archaeological sites in Utah are located in piñon-juniper woodland.

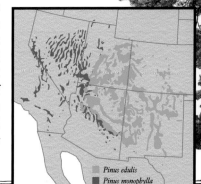

Pinus edulis
Pinus monophylla

Fremont Cottonwood
Populus fremontii

Found along the banks of rivers and streams in the Southwest U.S. and Mexico, water-loving cottonwoods are the tallest trees in Zion Canyon. In autumn their leaves turn gold, lighting up the park with brilliant foliage. In spring cottonwoods release millions of seeds covered in puffy white fibers. These "cotton" fibers gives the tree its name, and a single cottonwood can produce over 45 million fluffy seeds each year. Visit when the air is thick with cottonwood seeds and you might think it's snowing. The cotton acts like a sail, catching the wind and carrying the seed for miles. But cottonwood seeds will only germinate in the rarest of desert habitats: moist soil. Cottonwoods release millions of seeds in hopes that just a few will land along the banks of rivers or streams. The release of seeds coincides with spring floods, which saturate the soils along rivers. Unfortunately, cottonwoods in Zion Canyon suffer from a lack of flooding due to levees constructed in the 1930s to protect Zion Lodge and other buildings. The levees protected the buildings, but the lack of floods prevented new cottonwoods from taking root. The few seedlings that do sprout are often browsed by deer and other animals. To ensure healthy cottonwood populations moving forward, the park is planting and watering seedlings in Zion Canyon. Young trees have smooth, light bark that becomes deeply furrowed with age. Mature cottonwoods consume 30 or more gallons of water per day, and the largest trees can grow 100 feet or taller.

Ponderosa Pine
Pinus ponderosa

The most widely distributed pine species in North America, ponderosa pines grow from Canada to Mexico and are found in every state in the Western U.S. In Zion they prefer terraces and plateaus from 5,500 to 7,500 feet in elevation. Ponderosa pines are easily identified by their height (they can grow 150 feet or taller), long needles (up to eight inches in bundles of three), and thick, plate-like bark. If you still aren't sure, put your nose in the bark's cracks. If it smells like vanilla or butterscotch, it's a ponderosa pine. The tree is named for its heavy wood (*ponderosa* is Spanish for "heavy"), which is prized as lumber. Ponderosa pines can survive low-intensity fires thanks to thick bark, and mature trees are sometimes charred near the base. Far from a threat, small fires are essential to ponderosa health. Fire clears out competing species that would otherwise encroach on ponderosa habitat. Only enormous fires that burn the crown can kill a mature ponderosa. Older trees often drop lower branches to prevent fire from climbing the tree and reaching the crown. Ponderosas can even survive lightning strikes, which flash-boil the sap and blow off chunks of bark, sending energy away from the tree. As ponderosa pines grow older, the bark changes color. Young trees have black bark, while older trees have yellowish bark. Early settlers did not realize the black and yellow trunks belonged to the same species, which is why ponderosas pines are sometimes called blackjack pine or yellow pine. Under ideal conditions ponderosa pines can live 600 years or longer.

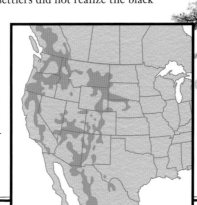

Cottonwoods in Autumn

Birds In Zion

Over 290 bird species have been identified in Zion, including 60 permanent residents and 100 species known to breed in the park. To learn more about birds in Zion, inquire at park visitor centers about the free "What's Flyin' in Zion" ranger program offered in the spring.

Peregrine Falcon
Falco peregrinus

Peregrine falcons are legendary hunters that can spot birds from thousands of feet above, then dive-bomb them at speeds topping 200 mph—the fastest speed of any animal. The collision creates an explosion of feathers, and victims that don't die upon impact have their necks broken by the peregrine's powerful beak. During World War II, Allied troops trained peregrine falcons to kill Nazi carrier pigeons. By the early 1970s, however, peregrine populations collapsed due to the toxic effects of the pesticide DDT. When ingested by birds, DDT fatally weakened eggshells, and mothers accidentally crushed their own brittle eggs. After DDT was banned, peregrine populations began to recover, and in 1999 peregrine falcons were removed from the federal endangered species list. Zion is home to roughly a dozen breeding peregrine pairs, which build their nests on sheer cliffs like Angels Landing.

Red-Tailed Hawk
Buteo jamaicensis

Named for their russet tail feathers, red-tailed hawks are skilled predators that can spot prey from hundreds of feet, then swoop down at speeds topping 120 mph. Powerful talons, which exert up to 200 pounds per square inch, grasp prey that includes squirrels, rabbits, lizards, snakes and birds. Red-tailed hawks sometimes emit a two- to three-second screechy *kree-eee-ar* that starts high and descends. Their wingspan measures nearly five feet across, and they can weigh up to 4.5 pounds. Males and females, which often mate for life, build stick nests that grow increasingly larger each year in tall trees or on high ledges.

Turkey Vulture
Cathartes aura

Turkey vultures are among the world's most successful scavengers, feeding on carrion (dead animals) detected using keen eyesight and a powerful sense of smell. Wingspans measuring up to six feet allow turkey vultures to soar over large areas in search of food. Their bald, featherless heads enable easy cleaning after poking around a bloody carcass. Turkey vultures (also called buzzards) range from Canada to Argentina. In Zion they are sometimes mistaken for California condors, but turkey vultures have white feathers on the outer edges of their wings while condors have black feathers on the outer edges of their wings. Both male and female turkey vultures are identical in plumage and similar in size. Adults weigh up to five pounds and can live 16 years in the wild.

Mexican Spotted Owl
Strix occidentalis lucida

These beautiful owls, one of three spotted owl subspecies in North America, range from the southern Rocky Mountains to central Mexico. In the 20th century, however, habitat loss led to steep population declines. By 1994 barely 2,000 Mexican spotted owls remained. Today, after decades of recovery efforts, Mexican spotted owls remain listed as a threatened species. In Zion, which is home to over 20 nesting pairs, owls nest in rocky canyons that offer cool shade in the desert. During the day they roost in trees or on rock ledges. At night they hunt small mammals. Large eyes provide superior vision in low light, but unlike most owls, which have yellow or orange eyes, Mexican spotted owls have dark eyes. Growing up to 19 inches long with a nearly four-foot wingspan, Mexican spotted owls are among the largest owls in North America. Adults can live about 15 years in the wild. Mating pairs are monogamous, and owlets less than five months old sport a soft, downy coat.

Mexican Spotted Owlet

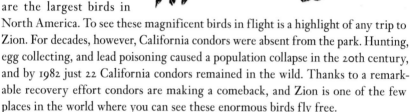

California Condor
Gymnogyps californianus

With a wingspan stretching up to 9.5 feet, California condors are the largest birds in North America. To see these magnificent birds in flight is a highlight of any trip to Zion. For decades, however, California condors were absent from the park. Hunting, egg collecting, and lead poisoning caused a population collapse in the 20th century, and by 1982 just 22 California condors remained in the wild. Thanks to a remarkable recovery effort condors are making a comeback, and Zion is one of the few places in the world where you can see these enormous birds fly free.

Although cursed with a face only a mother could love, California condors are exceptionally graceful in flight, riding thermals for hours without flapping their wings. They can soar as high as 15,000 feet and reach top speeds of 50 mph. In Zion, condors often become active around noon when thermal columns rise out of Zion Canyon. The area around Big Bend (p.164) is a particularly good place to spot condors. Although easily confused with turkey vultures, condors are significantly larger, with white "armpits" surrounded by black outer feathers. Turkey vultures, by contrast, have black armpits and white outer feathers. The two birds also have notably different flight patterns. Turkey vultures tend to fly in wobbly circles with their wings in a slight V-formation, while condors soar steady and smooth on outstretched wings.

Juvenile condors have black heads that turn pinkish-orange around age six. Mature condors weigh up to 23 pounds and can live 50 years or more. Like turkey vultures, California condors are scavengers that feed on carrion. A powerful bill breaks bones and tears flesh, while the bald head can dig deep into bloody carcasses without dirtying feathers. Condors prefer large mammals like elk, mule deer or cows, but they will eat just about any dead animal. Carrion availability is unreliable so condors eat as much as possible when they find a carcass. They store excess meat in a fleshy extension of their esophagus, called a "crop," that can hold more than three pounds of food.

California condors once ranged from Canada to Mexico. During the Ice Age, they feasted on the carcasses of large animals such as mammoths,

California Condor Range

mastodons and giant ground sloths. When those animals went extinct roughly 10,000 years ago, California condors lost a major source of food, and their population began to decline. By the time European explorers arrived, California condors were confined to western North America. By the 1940s, their range had shrunk to southern California.

In 1982, with worldwide populations of California condors down to just 22 birds, wildlife biologists took drastic steps to ensure the species' survival. They captured all remaining wild condors with cannon nets and transported them to the L.A. Zoo and the San Diego Wild Animal Park to begin a captive breeding program. The challenges were formidable. Condors do not reproduce until they are six years old, and mating pairs normally produce just one egg every other year. To stimulate egg production, biologists removed eggs as soon as they were laid, which tricked breeding condors into laying a second or even third egg. Extra eggs were incubated, and the first captive-bred California condor hatched in 1988. Biologists fed the incubated chicks with condor mother hand puppets, which prevented the birds from growing accustomed to humans.

In 1992, biologists released the first captive-bred condors in California. In 1996, six more condors were released at the Vermillion Cliffs in northern Arizona—the first time condors had flown free in Arizona since 1924. The birds soon discovered Grand Canyon and Zion, where rugged terrain and strong updrafts offer ideal conditions. Over the next two decades, as more captive-bred condors were released in the region, the number of California condors increased at both parks. In recent years Zion rangers have counted 42 condors at Lava Point!

Today there are almost 500 California condors. Nearly 300 live in the wild, including roughly 70 condors in Arizona and Utah. Although lead poisoning from spent bullets remains the biggest threat to wild condors, groups like the Peregrine Fund (peregrinefund.org) are working hard to ensure a bright future for these amazing birds.

Wild Turkey
Meleagris gallopavo

Wild turkeys are the same species as domestic turkeys cooked at Thanksgiving, but wild turkeys are divided into six distinct subspecies. Often traveling in flocks of 20 to 30 birds, wild turkeys eat nuts, berries and insects during the day, then roost in trees at night. In the spring, males puff out their tail feathers, swell their face wattles, and strut and gobble to attract females. Males often mate with multiple females, and they play no role raising the young. Adult turkeys, which can weigh 20 pounds or more, are among the heaviest birds in North America. Turkeys were first domesticated in Mexico around A.D. 500. Throughout the Southwest, native tribes raised turkeys for food and decorative feathers. Spanish explorers sent domestic turkeys to Europe in the early 1500s, and the English word "turkey" is likely derived from the country Turkey, which exported poultry to England. Prior to colonization there were an estimated ten million wild turkeys in America. By the early 20th century, however, hunting and habitat loss had reduced populations to perhaps 200,000—a 98% decline. Thanks to successful conservation efforts, wild turkey populations have rebounded to over six million birds.

Canyon Wren
Catherpes mexicanus

This small brown and white songbird is famous for its beautiful call, a series of delicate high-pitched whistles that descend in speed and tone. Spend a few days in Zion and you'll likely hear the canyon wren's melodic song echoing through the canyons. Nests are often built in rocky crevices, and males sing to defend their nesting territory. Canyon wrens are found in the mountains and canyons of the arid West, from British Columbia to southern Mexico. Their long, narrow bills are used to pluck insects and spiders from small openings and crevices. Canyon wrens, which are not known to drink water, are believed to get all of their liquids from insects.

Roadrunner
Geococcyx californianus

These long-legged birds are famously speedy.
Although unable to fly more than a few dozen
yards, roadrunners can reach top speeds of 20 mph on land
(faster than humans, but nearly half as fast as wily coyotes).
Highly maneuverable, roadrunners use their wings and
tail feathers as air rudders, allowing them to brake fast and execute tight turns.
They hunt insects and reptiles, including venomous lizards, scorpions and tarantula hawks. Roadrunners swallow horned lizards head-first with the lizard's horns
pointed away from the bird's vital organs. Perhaps most remarkably, roadrunners
hunt rattlesnakes by pinning the snake's head, bashing it against a rock, and swallowing the rattlesnake whole. If the snake is too long, a roadrunner swallows what
it can, letting the rest of the snake dangle from its mouth and swallowing bit by bit
as it digests. Found across the desert Southwest and northern Mexico, roadrunners
grow up to one foot high and two feet long. Their mottled brown plumage helps
them blend in with dusty desert shrubs.

American Dipper
Cinclus mexicanus

American dippers, sometimes called water
ouzels, are the only songbirds in America that spend
most of their time in and around water. You can often spot
these all-gray birds perched on rocks in a rushing stream.
American dippers can dive up to 20 feet underwater and stay
submerged for 30 seconds or more. While underwater, they use their wings to
"fly" in search of food such as insects, larvae, and small fish. An extra eyelid allows
American dippers to see underwater. The name "dipper" comes from the bird's habit
of bouncing up and down on river rocks. Some scientists believe dipping is a form
of communication that developed because bird calls are difficult to hear over the
sound of rushing water. To survive cold water in winter, dippers have low meta-
bolic rates and extra oxygen-carrying capacity in their blood. American dippers are
found in streams and rivers across much of the mountain West. They sometimes
build nests made of moss and twigs behind waterfalls, gaining access to the nest by
flying through the waterfall.

Desert Bighorn Sheep
Ovis canadensis nelsoni

Desert bighorn sheep are some of Zion's most impressive animals. Weighing up to 220 pounds, they are among the largest animals in the park—yet bighorns are extremely nimble for their size. Their concave hooves, which feature a hard outer edge and soft interior sole, grip rocks on sheer cliffs and steep, rocky terrain. Bighorns can navigate ledges two inches wide, scramble uphill at 15 mph, and jump down 20-foot inclines with grace. These skills, combined with keen eyesight and excellent hearing, help bighorns avoid predators such as mountain lions, bobcats and coyotes.

Native to the deserts of North America, desert bighorn sheep are a subspecies of bighorn sheep well-adapted to arid environments. Unlike Rocky Mountain bighorns, whose thick coat keeps them warm in the cold mountains, desert bighorns have short hair that helps dissipate heat. Desert bighorns also have smaller bodies and longer legs. They can survive weeks without water, deriving all of their moisture from plants. Grasses constitute the majority of their diet, but sedges and cacti sometimes provide additional calories. Bighorns have a complex nine-stage digestive process that maximizes removal of nutrients from food.

Both males (rams) and females (ewes) develop horns shortly after birth. The horns grow larger each year, and annual growth rings indicate a bighorn's age. Ewe horns never grow past half curl, but ram horns curve up and over the ears in a dramatic C-shaped curl. A mature ram's horns can weigh up to 30 pounds and measure up to three feet in length. If horns start to block peripheral vision they are deliberately "broomed" (rubbed down) on rocks. During mating season from July to October, competing rams charge each other head-on at speeds topping 20 mph. When rams collide, their horns smash together, producing a loud crack like a rifle shot that can often be

Historic Bighorn Range

Historic Desert Bighorn Range

heard for miles. Thickened skulls allow rams to withstand repeated collisions. Rams can fight for over 24 hours, and aggressive rams with the biggest horns generally do the most mating. Although rams are independent by nature, they range between herds of ewes during mating season. Unlike rams, ewes rarely venture far from their natal herd.

Ewes give birth to lambs from mid-January to April in Zion. Lactating ewes must drink water every day, and they often gather near permanent water sources during this time. Within a few weeks of birth, lambs separate from their mothers to form their own bands, seeking out mothers only to suckle. By six months lambs are completely weaned. But young bighorns remain vulnerable to predation, and only about one-third of desert bighorn lambs survive their first year. Lambs that survive to adulthood can live 20 years or more in the wild.

Desert bighorns are well adapted to drastic temperature fluctuations. In winter they are active during the day, but in summer they spend much of the day resting in the shade. Unlike most mammals, their body temperatures can safely fluctuate several degrees. During droughts they can lose up to 30% of their body weight. Bighorns often congregate near water sources during droughts, but this comes with great risk. Predators also gather near water sources, waiting for bighorns to descend from their steep hiding places to drink.

It has been estimated that over a million desert bighorn sheep once roamed the Southwest. According to Spanish explorers Dominguez and Escalante, who passed through the region in 1776, "Wild sheep breed ... in such abundance that the tracks look like those of great droves of tame sheep." But when settlers arrived in the mid-1800s, desert bighorn populations plummeted due to hunting and diseases transmitted by domestic sheep. By 1950 bighorn sheep had disappeared from Zion.

In 1978 the park initiated a desert bighorn recovery program. Biologists transported 14 sheep from Nevada to East Zion, hoping to reestablish a sustainable population. For the first few years the program did not go well, but in the 1980s the herd started to grow. Then, over the last decade, the population exploded to over 800 sheep—the healthiest population in Utah. Biologists now worry that Zion's bighorn herd has grown *too* large. As the herd spreads beyond Zion, it could come into contact with domestic sheep carrying deadly diseases. Efforts are now underway to transport some of Zion's herd to other parts of Utah where desert bighorn populations have yet to recover.

Desert Bighorn Lamb

Elk
Cervus canadensis

Elk are the largest animals in Zion. Females (cows) grow up to seven feet long and weigh up to 500 pounds, while males (bulls) grow up to eight feet long and weigh up to 800 pounds. Elk are the second-largest member of the deer family in North America. Only moose, which weigh up to 1,500 pounds, are larger. Elk are found at Zion's highest elevations such as Kolob Terrace.

Although similar to mule deer in appearance, elk are distinguished by their large size and distinct coloration: a tan body with a dark brown "pelage" (coat) above the neck. Shawnee Indians call elk *wapiti*, "white rump," because of its white back-sides. Only bulls have antlers, which can grow four feet long and weigh up to 40 pounds. Bulls shed their antlers each spring, and over the next three to four months new antlers grow back at the rate of about one-half inch per day, reaching maximum size in time for the fall rut (mating season).

During the rut, which lasts from late summer through fall, bulls emit a bugle-like sound as a sign of dominance and a challenge to other bulls. The bugle starts off as a bellow and changes to a shrill scream that can be heard for miles. Dominance between bulls is determined through antler clashes, and the most dominant bulls assemble a harem of a dozen or more cows. To attract females, bulls perfume themselves with their own urine. After a gestation period of roughly eight months, cows give birth to 35-pound newborns. Elk calves can stand within 20 minutes of birth, and they remain under their mothers's guidance for a full year.

Elk are ruminants with four-chambered stomachs. The first stomach stores food while the other three digest it. In summer, elk forage on grasses and leaves, and in winter they eat tree bark and twigs. Mature elk eat an average of 15 pounds of vegetation a day. With sufficient food elk can live 10 years or more in the wild.

By the early 1900s, elk had disappeared from the Southwest due to over-hunting. From 1912 to 1925, Utah imported elk from Yellowstone to reestablish local populations.

Mule Deer
Odocoileus hemionus

Mule deer are a common sight in Zion, often seen grazing in the early morning or late afternoon near campgrounds and Zion Lodge. Mule deer are named for their large ears, which move independently of one another like the ears of a mule. Common throughout the West, their range extends from western Canada to central Mexico. Females (does) weigh 95 to 200 pounds, while males (bucks) weigh 150 to 300 pounds.

Mule deer are slightly larger than white-tailed deer, to which they are closely related. Mule deer have white tails with a black tip, and their bifurcated antlers "fork" as they grow. (The antlers of white-tailed deer, by contrast, branch from a single main beam.) Bucks grow a large pair of antlers each year, then shed them each winter. This annual cycle of antler growth is regulated by changes in the length of the day.

Bucks compete for females during the fall rut, enmeshing their antlers and trying to force the head of the other buck down. Injuries are rare, but antlers sometimes become locked together. If two bucks cannot unlock their antlers to feed, both will eventually die of starvation.

After breeding in the fall, gestation lasts 190 to 200 days. Young does give birth to one fawn. Older does often give birth to twins. Fawns are born with white spots to help camouflage them with the dappled light of the forest floor, but as fawns grow older the spots disappear. Fawns can identify their mother through a unique odor produced by glands on the mother's hind legs. Fawns stay with their mothers until they are weaned in the fall. Conflict between does is common, so family groups tend to be spaced widely apart.

Mule deer are ruminants that ferment plants in their multi-chamber stomach before digestion. In summer they forage on plants, leaves and brushy vegetation. In winter they forage on conifers such as juniper and ponderosa pine. Gray winter fur is replaced in spring with a brown summer coat. Adult mule deer can live 11 years or more in the wild, but only if they avoid predators such as mountain lions, bobcats and coyotes.

Mule Deer
Range

Coyote
Canis latrans

Coyotes tend to be elusive during the day, but their haunting howls can echo through Zion at night. One long, high-pitched howl calls a pack together, and when the pack has gathered, a series of yips and yelps are often added to the mix. But coyotes have a reputation as tricksters, and what sounds like a large pack is sometimes just one or two coyotes making a variety of sounds to create the auditory illusion of a larger pack. Coyote vocalizations are surprisingly complex, with up to 11 distinct howls, yips, yaps and barks to communicate with one another.

Coyotes currently range from Canada to Panama, but historically they were confined to the open spaces of the Western U.S. and Mexico. Following the extermination of wolves in the 1800s, coyotes spread rapidly throughout North America. Intelligent, adaptable animals with a knack for scavenging, coyote populations have held steady and even increased in some places despite years of being hunted, poisoned and trapped.

Coyotes often travel in packs of six or so closely related family members. Their diet consists mostly of small mammals such as mice, squirrels and cottontails. Coyotes are highly opportunistic, however, and they will eat just about anything, including birds, snakes, insects and trash. Working in teams, coyotes sometimes hunt larger animals such as mule deer. While pursuing prey, they can reach top speeds of over 40 mph and jump 13 feet in length.

Coyotes mate in winter, and mothers give birth to an average of six pups in spring. Young coyotes are extremely vulnerable, and up to two-thirds of pups do not survive to adulthood. Those that survive their first year can often live ten years or more in the wild. Adult coyotes grow up to four feet in length and weigh up to 40 pounds. Desert coyotes, which weigh about half as much as other coyotes, have pale thin fur that helps dissipate heat.

Coyotes play a central role in the myths and legends of many native tribes, including the Southern Paiute. Among a cast of human/animal characters, the coyote is often portrayed as an intelligent, scheming trickster. The word "coyote" is derived from the Aztec word *cóyotl*. Coyote's Latin name, *Canis latrans*, means "barking dog."

Coyote Range

Mountain Lion
Felis concolor

Mountain lions (also called cougars, pumas, panthers and catamounts) are found from Canada to Argentina—the most extensive range of any mammal in the Western Hemisphere. Before European settlement, mountain lions inhabited all 48 lower U.S. states, but in the late 1800s and early 1900s they were hunted to the brink of extinction. Following the enactment of strict hunting regulations, mountain lions have made a steady comeback in the West, and they are now starting to spread to eastern states.

Mountain lions are the second-largest wildcats in the Western Hemisphere. Only jaguars are larger. Female mountain lions weigh up to 140 pounds and can measure up to seven feet in length. Males can weigh over 200 pounds and measure more than nine feet from nose to tail. Mountain lions have the largest proportional hind legs of any feline. They can jump nearly 20 feet vertically and 40 feet horizontally, and they can run up to 50 mph. Retractable claws aid in both hunting and tree climbing.

Mountain lions travel up to 25 miles a day in search of food, killing prey every four to eight days. Excellent night vision enables them to hunt from dusk till dawn. They are quick, efficient hunters that quietly stalk prey before pouncing. Victims often die from a lethal bite to the spinal cord. Mule deer are mountain lions preferred prey in Zion, constituting up to 90% of their diet. Mountain lions also hunt elk and bighorn sheep, as well as smaller animals like squirrels and rodents.

Solitary and territorial, mountain lions require an extensive home range of up to 300 square miles. Adult mountain lions come together only to mate. Females are exclusively responsible for parenting, and cubs stay with mothers for roughly two years while learning survival skills. Mountain lion pups are born with spots, but they develop a uniform tan coloration by about 2.5 years in age.

Reclusive by nature, mountain lions go to great lengths to avoid people. Sightings are rare in Zion, and there has never been a fatal human attack in the park. If you do encounter a mountain lion, slowly back away while holding a steady gaze.

Mountain Lion Range

Ringtail Cat
Bassariscus astutus

One of Zion's most adorable and elusive mammals, ringtail cats are nocturnal creatures with big eyes and fluffy tails. Although they have many feline characteristics—agility, semi-retractable claws, impressive climbing skills—they are not technically cats. They belong to the procyonid family that includes raccoons. Legend has it that miners once kept ringtails as pets to hunt mice and rodents, hence the colloquial name "miners cat." Ringtail cats weigh about two pounds and can measure over two feet long. Their tail, which is covered in black and white rings, is about 12 inches in length. Large eyes provide excellent night vision to hunt rodents, lizards and other small animals. Although mostly carnivorous, ringtail cats are omnivores that also eat berries and fruits. They are highly adept at escaping predators such as owls, hawks and bobcats, releasing a foul-smelling secretion when threatened. The ringtail cat range extends from southern Oregon throughout much of the Southwest, including parts of Texas and Mexico.

Bobcat
Lynx rufus

Ranging from Southwestern deserts to the swamps of Florida, bobcats are North America's most common wildcat. But they are highly elusive animals and rarely seen. Bobcats typically spend the day resting, becoming active around dusk to search for prey. Their diet includes a wide range of small animals such as rabbits, squirrels, birds and snakes. Rather than chase prey, bobcats prefer seeking out a hiding spot and lying in wait. When a victim approaches, the bobcat pounces, snagging its prey with sharp, retractable claws. Bobcats share many personality traits with housecats, including hissing, purring and using trees as scratching posts. But with an average weight of 20 pounds, bobcats are nearly double the size of housecats. Like most felines, bobcats are largely solitary. Males and females come together only to mate. Females generally have litters of two or three kittens, and those that reach adulthood typically live six to eight years in the wild.

Jackrabbit
Lepus californicus

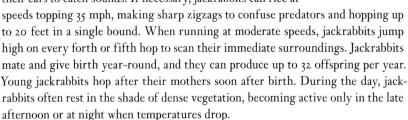

Found throughout much of the American West and northern Mexico, jackrabbits were originally called "jackass rabbits" by early settlers because of their large, donkey-like ears. Jackrabbits have highly advanced senses and reflexes to avoid predators such as coyotes, bobcats and owls. Giant ears give them exceptional hearing, and their eyes are pushed so far apart that they have almost full, 360-degree vision. When alarmed, jackrabbits freeze to avoid detection, moving only their ears to catch sounds. If necessary, jackrabbits can flee at speeds topping 35 mph, making sharp zigzags to confuse predators and hopping up to 20 feet in a single bound. When running at moderate speeds, jackrabbits jump high on every forth or fifth hop to scan their immediate surroundings. Jackrabbits mate and give birth year-round, and they can produce up to 32 offspring per year. Young jackrabbits hop after their mothers soon after birth. During the day, jackrabbits often rest in the shade of dense vegetation, becoming active only in the late afternoon or at night when temperatures drop.

Desert Cottontail
Sylvilagus audubonii

Named for their puffy white tails, desert cottontails range from eastern Montana to central Mexico. Adults grow up to 17 inches long and weigh up to 3.3 pounds. Strict vegetarians, desert cottontails feed primarily on grasses, but they will also nibble on shrubs and cacti. Like most rabbits, cottontails re-ingest their own feces to extract maximum nutrition from food. Desert cottontails are most active in the early morning and late afternoon, preferring to spend the hot midday hours resting in shady burrows. To save energy they often use burrows made by other rodents instead of making their own. Cottontail predators include coyotes, bobcats and mountain lions. Due to their relative abundance and high reproductive rate, desert cottontails were an important resource for native tribes, who ate their meat and used their soft pelts to make warm blankets.

Beavers
Castor canadensis

Weighing up to 90 pounds, beavers are the largest rodents in North America. They use their large incisors to gnaw on tree trunks and topple trees that, in most places, would be used to build dams and lodges. But Zion's beavers are different. The Virgin River floods so frequently that Zion's beavers don't even try to build dams. Instead, they live in earthen dens in the river banks, earning them the nickname "bank beavers." Well-adapted to their aquatic environment, beavers can stay underwater for up to 15 minutes and swim half a mile before coming up for air. Large, webbed hind feet aid in swimming, and flat tails are used as rudders. On land, beavers prop themselves up on their tails while gnawing on trees—a habit they retain in Zion for good dental hygiene. The beaver's thick fur coat was so prized by early European trappers that beavers were hunted out of much of their natural range. In the early 1900s, laws were enacted to protect beaver populations. Since then, North American beaver populations have recovered to roughly 10–15 million—a fraction of the estimated 100–200 million present before Columbus.

Yellow-bellied Marmot
Marmota flaviventris

These roly-poly rodents (western cousins of groundhogs and woodchucks) are generally found at elevations above 6,500 feet. In summer, they gorge on leaves, grasses, berries, flowers, insects, and bird eggs, packing on as much fat as possible to survive the harsh winter ahead. By autumn, marmots can weigh up to 12 pounds. During hibernation, their body temperature drops from 97°F to 40°F, their heartbeat drops to four beats per minute, and they breathe just once every six minutes. In spring, after emerging from hibernation, male marmots dig new dens under rock piles and gather a harem of up to four females. Female marmots have litters of three to five pups, but only about half survive their first year. Adult marmots can live up to 15 years.

Squirrels & Chipmunks

Say hello to Zion's most dangerous wild animals. Some visitors worry about mountain lions or rattlesnakes, but squirrels and chipmunks are actually the number one cause of human-animal injuries in Zion. Unlike rattlesnakes and mountain lions, which are smart enough to avoid people, some people are not smart enough to avoid squirrels and chipmunks. Instead, they approach the adorable critters and offer them food. The rodents respond by biting the person's hand, resulting in blood, stitches or even disease. Squirrels and chipmunks also chew through unattended backpacks and tents when they smell food inside.

Rock Squirrel

There are five squirrel species in Zion National Park, but rock squirrels (*Spermophilus variegatus*) are the most common. Grayish-brown with patches of cinnamon, rock squirrels are the largest squirrels in Zion, growing up to 21 inches long. As their name implies, they prefer rocky habitat. Smaller ground squirrels in Zion include the golden-mantled ground squirrel (*Callospermophilus lateralis*) and white-tailed antelope squirrel (*Ammospermophilus leucurus*), both of which have white stripes running down their sides. Red squirrels (*Tamiasciurus hudsonicus*) are tree squirrels that feed on conifers growing at the park's higher elevations. The northern flying squirrel (*Glaucomys sabrinus*), one of just two flying squirrel species in North America, can glide up to 70 feet between trees thanks to a fold of skin between its wrist and ankle.

Chipmunks are smaller than squirrels, rarely growing longer than 10 inches. Both squirrels and chipmunks can have stripes running down their sides, but only chipmunks have stripes on their faces. There are three chipmunk species in Zion: the Uinta chipmunk (*Neotamias umbrinus*), which holds its tail up when it runs, the least chipmunk (*Neotamias minimus*) and the cliff chipmunk (*Neotamias dorsalis*), which swing their tails side to side when they run. The least chipmunk is the smallest chipmunk in North America, weighing less than 2.5 ounces.

Squirrels and chipmunks are mostly herbivores, but they are opportunists that will eat just about anything, including insects, bird eggs and small vertebrates. Squirrels and chipmunks are preyed upon, in turn, by hawks, owls and mountain lions.

Uinta Chipmunk

Gila Monster
Heloderma suspectum

The largest lizards in North America, Gila monsters grow up to two feet long and weigh up to four pounds. Their range extends from the Mojave Desert in southwest Utah to the Sonoran and Chihuahuan deserts in northwest Mexico. In Zion they are found in the arid lowlands near the southern boundary of the park. Gila (pronounced *HEE-la*) monsters are the only venomous lizards native to the United States, but they are slow, sluggish animals that pose little threat to humans. The name "Gila" refers to the Gila River in Arizona, where the lizards were first discovered. The "monster" epithet likely comes from the exaggerated beliefs of early settlers, who claimed the lizard had a poisonous breath, vice-like jaws, and a fatal bite. Although no deaths have ever been confirmed from Gila monsters, their venom is among the most painful of any reptile, once described as "hot lava coursing through your veins." Gila monsters prey on small birds, mammals and insects, and they are fond of bird and reptile eggs. Gila monster predators include coyotes and hawks. The lizard's scientific name *Heloderma* means "studded skin," and their bright pink or yellow coloration likely serves as a defensive warning.

Great Basin Collared Lizard
Crotaphytus bicinctores

This medium-sized lizard, also known as the Mojave black-collared lizard or desert collared lizard, is famous for its beautiful markings, a combination of earth tone dots, spots and two black "collars" on the neck. The top collar wraps partway around the neck of females and completely around the neck of males. Great Basin collared lizards can grow up to a foot long from snout to tail. Their tail is often twice as long as their body. The lizards live in rocky, arid regions from southeastern Oregon and western Idaho to southern California and western Arizona. In mid-morning they are often seen basking on top of rocks, which serve as lookouts for prey. Great Basin collared lizards eat insects, spiders and small lizards, as well as leaves and flowers.

Chuckwalla
Sauromalus ater

The second-largest lizards in North America (after Gila monsters), chuckwallas are members of the iguana family with round bellies, thick tails, and loose folds of skin around the neck and shoulders. They can measure up to 20 inches in length and weigh up to two pounds. Chuckwallas range from southern Utah to northern Mexico and the Baja Peninsula. After a cold night in the desert, chuckwallas bask in the morning sun until their body temperature reaches 100°F, at which point they search for food. Strict vegetarians, they browse on leaves, buds, flowers and fruit. When threatened or frightened, chuckwallas retreat to rocky crevices, wedging themselves in place by inflating their lungs up to three times normal breathing capacity. Southwestern tribes, who hunted chuckwallas and considered its meat a delicacy, would puncture the inflated lizard with a sharp stick to remove it from its hiding place. Chuckwallas mate in spring, and females lay clutches of five to ten eggs in summer. Males defend their territory through physical displays including push-ups, head-bobbing and gaping of the mouth.

Desert Horned Lizard

Horned Lizards

These lizards, sometimes called horny toads, look like mini-dinosaurs with pointy horns and spines covering their head and back. The horns and spines deter predators by making the lizards hard to swallow. If that doesn't work, the greater short-horned lizard (*Phyrnosoma hernandesi*) can shoot foul-smelling blood up to six feet from its eyes to startle and confuse predators. The greater short-horned lizard grows up to five inches long and ranges from southern Canada to central Mexico. The desert horned lizard (*Phrynosoma platyrhinos*) grows up to five inches long and ranges from southern Idaho to northern Mexico. Horned lizards are sit-and-wait predators that feed primarily on harvester ants and are often found near ant hills. Additional prey includes grasshoppers, crickets and beetles.

Greater Short-horned Lizard

Mojave Desert Tortoise
Gopherus agassizii

Growing up to 14 inches long and weighing up to 50 pounds, Mojave desert tortoises are the largest reptiles in Zion. They are found in the low elevation deserts near the park's southern boundary, which marks the northeast limit of their range. From Zion their range extends across northwest Arizona and southern Nevada into southern California.

Desert tortoises spend up to 95 percent of their time underground, where temperatures are cooler in summer and warmer in winter. Using sharp claws they dig burrows up to six feet deep. Desert tortoises hibernate in winter and spend much of summer in a semi-dormant state. They are most active after seasonal rains, when they have the rare opportunity to rehydrate. Desert tortoises can store up to 40% of their body weight as water in their bladders. Strict vegetarians, they can also obtain water from foods such as grasses, flowers and cacti. In extreme cases desert tortoises can survive a full year without drinking water.

Desert tortoises have a maximum speed of about 0.2 mph, and they rarely wander more than a few miles from their birthplace. When two tortoises meet, they engage in a series of rituals that can include circling one another, head bobbing, chin sniffing and biting. Males sometimes engage in aggressive jostling, using their gular horn (a hard protrusion on the front underside of their shell) to try to flip their opponent over. If an overturned tortoise cannot flip itself right side up, it will die of suffocation or exposure.

Desert tortoises mate year-round, and females can retain sperm for up to a decade and still lay fertile eggs. Females lay an average of five eggs, which hatch 70 to 120 days later. Incubation temperatures determine whether the eggs will develop into males or females. Juvenile desert tortoises, which have soft shells, are extremely vulnerable to predators such as ravens and Gila monsters. Tortoises that survive to adulthood can live over half a century.

Sadly, Mojave desert tortoises are listed as endangered due to a variety of modern threats. As more people have moved to the Southwest, desert tortoise populations have declined due to habitat loss, disease and vehicle strikes. If you a encounter a desert tortoise, do not disturb it. Frightened tortoises often empty their bladders, robbing them of a crucial water source.

Mojave Desert
Tortoise Range

Zion Snail
Physa Zionis

The Zion snail, which lives only in The Narrows (p.184) and along Riverside Walk (p.169), is barely the size of a pinhead, measuring between one-sixteenth and one-eighth of an inch long. For years this minuscule mollusk was believed to be world's smallest snail, but a snail recently discovered in China is smaller. The Zion snail has a streamlined shell and an unusually large foot-to-body ratio, which helps it cling to rocks during flash floods. While exploring Riverside Walk or The Narrows, keep your eyes out for these tiny black specks near seeps and springs.

Canyon Tree Frog
Hyla arenicolor

There are six species of frogs and toads in Zion, but the canyon tree frog is arguably the park's most famous amphibian. Its surprisingly loud mating call, which is often compared to bleating sheep, can be heard at water sources in spring and summer. Growing just over two inches long, canyon tree frogs are often easier to hear than see. Their tan-gray coloration provides excellent camouflage against Zion's rocks, and during dry spells they take refuge in rocky crevices.

Virgin River Fish

Six fish species are native to the Virgin River Basin, four of which live in Zion. All evolved to live in muddy rivers with frequent floods and dramatic temperature fluctuations. Thanks to the Virgin River's natural, undammed flow, which clears out non-native fish during floods, Zion has some of the healthiest native fish populations in the Southwest. The speckled dace (*Rhinichthys osculus*) is a small minnow common in rivers west of the Rocky Mountains. The flannelmouth sucker (*Catostomus latipinnis*), which grows up to two feet long, has healthy populations in Zion but is extirpated below Lake Mead. The Virgin spinedace (*Lepidomeda mollispinis mollispinis*) grows up to six inches long and is similar in appearance to a trout. The desert sucker (*Catostomus clarkii*) grows up to 15 inches.

Speckled Dace

Western
Rattlesnake

Snakes

Zion is home to 13 snake species, most of which are nocturnal and rarely encountered during the day. Zion's only venomous snake, the western rattlesnake (*Crotalus oreganus*), goes out of its way to avoid people. When threatened, it uses its namesake rattle as a warning to keep away. The rattle, which grows larger each time the snake sheds its skin, is made of interlocking segments of keratin, the same material found in human hair and fingernails. Growing four feet or longer, western rattlesnakes patiently lie in wait for small mammals and birds, detecting prey through infrared sensors and a keen sense of smell. When the rattler strikes, sharp fangs inject a paralyzing venom into the victim, which is swallowed head-first and digested over several days. Western rattlesnakes, in turn, are preyed upon by owls and hawks, which kill snakes by plucking them from the ground and repeatedly dropping them from the air. Another rattlesnake predator in Zion is the common kingsnake (*Lampropeltis getula*), a powerful constrictor that suffocates victims by wrapping tightly around their bodies. Common kingsnakes are easily identified by their black and white bands.

Common
Kingsnake

Black Widow Spider
Latrodectus hesperus

The most venomous spiders in North America, black widows are found across much of the continent, including Utah, which is home to the western black widow. The jet black female is easily identified by bright coloration on her half-inch abdomen. Males have a tan coloration and are less than half the size of females. Female black widows have unusually large venom glands, which they use to subdue prey. The bite, while painful, is rarely fatal in humans. Despite their name and reputation, female western black widows rarely eat males after mating—although males do show a preference for mating with females who have recently eaten.

Tarantula

Tarantulas are the largest spiders in the world, and in Zion they can measure up to eight inches long. Covered with thousands of sensitive hairs that detect the motion of nearby prey, tarantulas eat anything they can chase down, including beetles, grasshoppers, lizards and small mammals. Once captured, prey is injected with paralyzing venom, and a digestive enzyme is secreted to liquefy the victim's internal organs. The tarantula then sucks out the organ soup with its straw-like mouth. (Tarantula bites, it should be noted, are painful but harmless to humans.) Tarantulas are most active during fall mating season, when male tarantulas wander in search of female burrows.

Tarantula Hawk
Pepsis formosa

This large wasp, which grows up to two inches long, is a tarantula's worst nightmare. After stinging a tarantula with paralyzing venom, a female tarantula hawk drags the spider back to its burrow, lays her eggs on its body, and seals the burrow—effectively burying the spider alive. When the wasp larvae hatch, they feast on the still-living tarantula, munching on non-essential body parts first to maximize freshness by keeping the spider alive as long as possible.

Scorpions

Zion is home to the largest scorpion in the United States—the giant desert hairy scorpion, which grows up to five inches long—as well as the most venomous scorpion in North America—the bark scorpion, whose sting causes severe pain for up to 72 hours. Fortunately, scorpions are nocturnal creatures not often encountered, and their sting is rarely fatal. Scorpion eyes are exceptionally sensitive in low light, and they detect prey by sensing tiny vibrations on the ground. Their famous stinger, located at the tip of the tail, is thrust over the head to stab victims and inject venom when prey cannot be subdued with pincers alone. Scorpion prey includes insects and lizards. Scorpions are preyed upon, in turn, by coyotes, owls and roadrunners.

Giant Desert Hairy Scorpion

Southgate Petroglyphs near Zion's South Entrance

HISTORY

THE FIRST EVIDENCE of humans in Utah dates back roughly 10,000 years, toward the end of the last Ice Age. As temperatures warmed, nomadic hunter-gatherers wandered into a semi-arid landscape that was wetter and greener than today. They hunted animals with stone-tipped spears, wove baskets and nets, and ground seeds and nuts on stone metates. As the climate dried out, they adapted by harvesting a wide variety of native plants and animals.

Starting around 1000 B.C., a new culture called the Ancestral Puebloans (Anasazi) appeared in the Four Corners Region. (*Anasazi* is a Navajo word that means "Ancient Enemies" which modern descendants of Ancestral Puebloans do not appreciate.) Within a few centuries, Ancestral Puebloans had become one of the most advanced civilizations in America. They hunted with bows and arrows and made elaborate painted pottery. In New Mexico they built impressive cliff dwellings and six-story stone structures. (These structures were the tallest buildings in America until skyscrapers appeared in the 1880s.)

In Zion, which was located near the western outskirts of Ancestral Puebloan territory, construction was far more modest. One-story houses and storage units were built above the banks of the Virgin River, where the Virgin Branch of Ancestral Puebloans took up residence around 2,000 years ago.

Ancestral Puebloans flourished thanks to agriculture—specifically beans, corn and squash, which were first domesticated in Mexico. These crops, called the "Three Sisters," provide high nutrition and grow well together. Corn stalks provide structure for beans, beans fix nitrogen in the soil, and squash leaves deter pests while providing shade to keep soil moist. Farms were located near dependable water sources, often with irrigation ditches.

Over the centuries, Ancestral Puebloans grew less reliant on wild food and more reliant on agriculture. Decades of increased precipitation boosted harvests, increased population, and accelerated the transition to a semi-sedentary lifestyle. It also left Ancestral Puebloans vulnerable to climate change.

Starting around A.D. 1000, a series of multi-decade droughts devastated Ancestral Puebloan society. Environmental stress and crop failure led to social collapse and civilizational decline. By A.D. 1300, Ancestral Puebloans, including the Virgin Branch, had abandoned much of their territory.

Native Objects

Projectile Points

Both Ancestral Puebloan and Southern Paiute men hunted with bows and arrows, a technology that arrived in the Southwest around 2,000 years ago. Ancestral Puebloans fashioned projectile points from petrified wood found in Chinle Formation rocks. The Southern Paiute poisoned projectile points with venom from rattlesnakes and crushed black widow spiders.

Stone Grinders

Native tribes used stone grinding tools like mortars and pestles (pictured) and manos and metates to grind nuts, grains and seeds into flour. Cultivated maize was a major food source for Ancestral Puebloans. The Southern Paiute gathered large quantities of piñon pine nuts.

Baskets & Jugs

Basketmaking was an essential skill for Southern Paiute women, who wove plant fibers into a wide variety of objects—from cooking vessels to storage containers to hats. Pine pitch was used to waterproof woven water jugs like the one pictured here.

Pottery

Clay pottery allowed Ancestral Puebloans to place cooking vessels directly into fire to boil liquids and make soups. The Southern Paiute, by contrast, did not make pottery, preferring to boil liquids by dropping hot rocks into tightly woven baskets. Pottery is heavy and fragile, a technology better-suited to semi-sedentary people, like the Ancestral Puebloans, than the highly mobile Southern Paiute.

Sandals

Both Ancestral Puebloans and Southern Paiute fashioned clothes and footwear from yucca fiber. This woven sandal, which dates between A.D. 700 and 1100, was found at an Ancestral Puebloan archaeological site in the park.

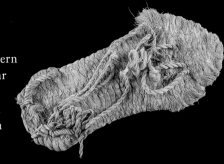

Winnowing Baskets

Southern Paiute women used winnowing baskets to separate piñon pine nuts from their shells. During the annual piñon harvest, pine nuts were roasted in their shells, crushed using stone grinders, and placed in winnowing baskets. Women then skillfully flicked nuts and shells in the air to blow away the lighter shells.

Wikiups

The Southern Paiute once lived in traditional shelters made of wooden poles lashed together with animal sinew. The frame was covered with brush, woven willows, strips of juniper bark or rabbit skins. A fire in the center of the wikiup kept people warm, and a hole in the roof allowed smoke to escape.

SOUTHERN PAIUTE

A few centuries before Ancestral Puebloans left Zion, the Southern Paiute arrived. This Numic-speaking group migrated from southern California to Utah around A.D. 1000. They likely interacted with Ancestral Puebloans, but whether as friends or enemies remains unclear.

The Southern Paiute refer to themselves as *Nuwuvi*, "the People." Their homeland includes southern Utah and Nevada, northern Arizona, and parts of eastern California. Covering 30 million acres, it encompasses both the Mojave Desert and the Great Basin Desert. Although resources seem limited, this region is dotted with forested plateaus and high elevation peaks that can receive five times more precipitation than the hot, dry lowlands. By moving seasonally through a variety of elevations, the Southern Paiute enjoyed a tremendous variety of edible plants and wild game. In years when favorite foods were scarce, they had plenty of alternatives. Their flexible, nomadic lifestyle was a sharp contrast to the semi-sedentary Ancestral Puebloans, and it could explain why the Southern Paiute survived in the same environment the Ancestral Puebloans abandoned.

Throughout spring and summer, the Southern Paiute followed ripening cycles to progressively higher elevations. Because water was scarce, they knew the location of every spring and seep, no matter how small. The Southern Paiute set up temporary camps near water sources and lived in domed *wikiups* made from branches and bushes. In the few places where water was plentiful, such as the Virgin River, they cultivated beans, corn and squash (a practice they may have learned from Ancestral Puebloans). Harvests were limited, however, and farming never replaced wild food as a primary nutrition source.

Although Southern Paiutes adapted well to the arid environment, there was rarely abundance. Limited resources kept most groups small, with an average of three to five households. Different groups went by different names. The *Unkaka'niguts* ("Red-Cliff-Base People") lived near Bryce Canyon, the *Pagu'its* ("Fish People") lived near Panguitch Lake, and the *Ea'ayekunants* ("Arrow Quiver People") lived near the Virgin River.

Daily responsibilities were defined by gender. Men hunted deer and rabbits with bows and arrows. Birds, bugs and worms provided additional protein, and chuckwalla was considered a delicacy. Women harvested seeds and roots with specialized tools and stored them in tightly woven baskets. Southern Paiute women were such accomplished weavers that some baskets held water.

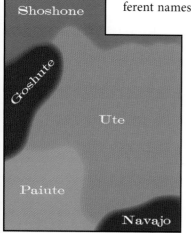

UTAH TRIBES

Tightly woven cooking baskets, into which women dropped hot rocks to boil liquids, required the greatest skill to make.

One of the most important foods was piñon pine nuts, which were harvested in autumn when pine cones open. Boys climbed piñon pines to shake out the cones, men beat the branches with long sticks, girls and women gathered cones and nuts on the ground, and grandmothers cleaned the nuts for roasting. Women then broke the outer shells with manos and metates (grinding stones) and separated the shells from the nuts using a winnowing basket. The annual piñon pine harvest was celebrated with feasting, singing and dancing.

Women made clothes out of animal skins and plant fibers. A favorite technique was rolling fur around yucca fiber, then sewing the fibers together to make warm, fuzzy blankets. Yucca fibers were also used for ropes, sandals, baskets and mats. Yucca root was diced and soaked in water to make soap and shampoo.

The Southern Paiute believe in an all-powerful spirit (the "one who made the earth") embodied by a variety of natural phenomenon, most notably the sun. Sunrise and sunset are often times of prayer. Other mythic heroes include the virtuous Sinawava (Wolf) and his trickster younger brother Kinesava (Coyote). There are also Thunder People, who inhabit the sky, and Water Babies, who live in springs, rivers and lakes. Southern Paiute shaman, called *paugant*, are guided by spirit animals to both heal the sick and curse enemies.

In the Southern Paiute worldview everything in nature is alive, including rocks, water and air—and all must be treated with respect. The Southern Paiute believe it is their duty to care for both nature and its spirits on earth.

EARLY EXPLORERS

On July 29, 1776, two Spanish friars left Santa Fe in present-day New Mexico and headed north. The goal of 36-year-old Fray Francisco Atanasio Domínguez and 26-year-old Fray Francisco Silvestre Vélez de Escalante was to find a route to the new mission in Monterey, California. Because Hopi land west of Santa Fe was considered unsafe, the friars opted for a northern route through Spain's vast, unexplored territory.

The Domínguez-Escalante expedition, which consisted of 13 men on horseback, including three native guides, rode up western Colorado and across northeast Utah. By early October, however, the mountains were covered in snow. Recognizing the peril that lay ahead, the men called off the expedition and headed back to Santa Fe. Along the way they passed within 20 miles of Zion Canyon. Escalante described the Paiutes they encountered as "of pleasing appearance, very friendly and extremely timid."

It would be another half century before white men set foot in the region again. After Mexico declared independence from Spain in 1821, American mountain men began trickling across the Western frontier. In 1826, fur trapper Jedediah Smith led an expedition across Utah in search of beaver, whose eastern populations had plummeted due to a fad for beaver pelt hats. Smith passed close to Zion and remarked that Utah's tribes were "cleanly quiet and active and make a nearer approach to civilized life than any Indians I have seen in the Interior."

Around 1830 a route called the Old Spanish Trail connected Santa Fe to Los Angeles, and large caravans began passing through southern Utah. The caravans traded blankets from Santa Fe for horses and mules in Los Angeles—and acquired slaves along the way.

The Old Spanish Trail, which passed within sight of Zion's Kolob Canyons, dramatically altered the lives of the region's tribes. There were exciting new trade opportunities, but not all of them were positive. The Ute, who acquired horses from the Spanish, raided Southern Paiute villages, taking women and children as slaves. The Southern Paiute, whose territory did not have adequate grazing for horses, found themselves at a strategic disadvantage—not only from Ute horseback raiders to the north, but also from Navajo horseback raiders to the east.

The most devastating impact, however, came from previously unknown European diseases. Smallpox, measles, cholera and influenza devastated native populations, which had virtually no immunity. By some estimates, disease killed up to 90 percent of native tribes in the centuries following European contact.

Meanwhile, another drastic change loomed on the horizon. In 1848 the United States emerged victorious in the Mexican-American War, which was triggered by the secession of Texas from Mexico. In exchange for 18 million dollars, the U.S. acquired nearly one million square miles including the future states of California, Arizona, Nevada, Utah, New Mexico and Colorado.

Suddenly, the United States stretched across North America. Over the next few decades, however, most activity was concentrated in California, where the Gold Rush lured thousands of fortune seekers. Utah, with its arid climate, lack of mineral wealth, and physically challenging terrain, was a place that no one wanted to settle—which is exactly what attracted the Mormons.

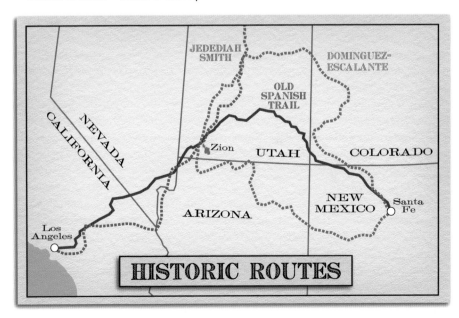

MORMON SETTLERS

In 1823, an 18-year-old named Joseph Smith received angelic visions in upstate New York. Seven years later he published the Book of Mormon and founded a new religion—a "purified" form of Christianity—which some considered a cult. To avoid persecution, Smith and his followers headed west—first Missouri, then Ohio, then Illinois—encountering hostility everywhere they went. In 1844, while Smith was imprisoned in Carthage, Illinois, an angry mob stormed the jail and murdered him.

Brigham Young, one of Smith's lieutenants, took over the Mormon church. Determined to fulfill Smith's vision of establishing an "American Zion," Young led 10,000 followers beyond the Western frontier. On July 29, 1847, they reached an enormous salt lake in the desert, called *Pi'a-pa* ("Big Water") by local tribes. Young took one look at the desolate scenery and declared: "This is the right place."

Salt Lake City, as Young called it, still belonged to Mexico, but Grand Canyon provided a natural barrier between Mexicans and Mormons. Young dreamed of creating an independent republic, much like Texas, but within a year the region fell under U.S. control. In 1851 Congress created the territory of Utah, and Brigham Young was named its first governor.

Mormons quickly radiated out from Salt Lake City. In 1853, church elders sent 50 missionaries to settle southern Utah on the banks of the Virgin River. There, on the advice of Mormons from Southern states, they planted cotton. The cotton flourished, and the region became known as "Utah Dixie."

Mormon settlers eagerly cultivated friendships with the Southern Paiute. The Book of Mormon teaches that American Indians are descended from a lost tribe of Israel that crossed the Atlantic in boats around 600 B.C. Although God eventually cursed these dark-skinned "Lamanites" for bad behavior, upon accepting Christianity they would become a "delightsome people" who would help usher in the second coming of Jesus. Not surprisingly, many Mormons viewed befriending and converting native tribes as a religious duty.

In 1858 Brigham Young directed Nephi Johnson, a young missionary and Indian interpreter, to explore the upper reaches of the Virgin River. Johnson hired Southern Paiutes to guide him upriver, where he became the first white man to enter Zion Canyon. In 1862, Albert Petty settled by a large spring near the mouth of Zion Canyon, which his wife named "Springdale." When the Civil War threatened Utah's cotton supply, Young dispatched hundreds of Mormons to southern Utah, and Springdale was soon home to nearly two dozen families.

One of the new arrivals, Isaac Behunin, built a summer cabin in Zion Canyon in 1863. Behunin, who was once Joseph Smith's bodyguard, was a regular smoker, and it was rumored that he was drawn to the canyon by its native tobacco. It was Behunin who coined the name "Zion," declaring it a place of refuge should Mormons ever be persecuted again.

CULTURE CLASH

When Mormons first arrived in Southern Paiute territory the two groups enjoyed a cautious peace. The Southern Paiute benefited from increased trade and Mormon protection against Ute and Navajo raiders. But as more Mormons arrived, relations began to sour.

One of the biggest problems was livestock, which displaced wild animals and consumed plants central to the native diet. In response, some Southern Paiute hunted cattle. As one observer put it, "The white man hunted the Indians' deer so why should not the Indian hunt the white man's cattle?" Mormons responded by providing Southern Paiute with food rations. According to Brigham Young, "it was better to feed the Indians than fight them."

Unfortunately, tensions of all kinds were on the rise. In September 1857, a Mormon militia slaughtered over 100 California-bound migrants at Mountain Meadow, just north of present-day St. George. The militia dressed in native clothes in an attempt to pin the blame on local tribes.

The motivation behind the Mountain Meadows Massacre remains unclear, but it occurred during a tense confrontation between Mormons and federal troops. President James Buchanan, concerned that Utah was going rogue, dispatched troops to the territory in 1857. Mormons assumed they were once again under assault. Although tension between Mormons and Washington eventually subsided, tensions between Mormons and natives continued to rise.

By 1859, Mormons had established nearly a dozen settlements in Southern Paiute territory. The settlers always took the best land, and the power balance soon shifted in their favor. In 1865, some Southern Paiute and Navajo joined forces with Ute war chief Black Hawk in a desperate attempt to reclaim their sovereignty. A three-year conflict ensued, and despite Mormon requests for federal troops that were repeatedly ignored, the Mormons emerged victorious.

The Black Hawk War forced the Utes onto the Uintah reservation east of Salt Lake City. The Southern Paiute, however, refused to leave their homeland. Although Southern Paiutes ultimately provided the largest number of Mormon converts of any Utah tribe, problems continued to flare. In 1869 Rockville settler Tom Flanigan fatally shot a Southern Paiute man. The tribe demanded that Flanigan surrender to be tortured and killed, but the settlers refused. Eventually, after lengthy negotiations, the Southern Paiute accepted an ox as retribution.

The Buckskin Apostle

JACOB HAMBLIN

Few people did more to alleviate conflict between Southwestern tribes and white settlers than Jacob Hamblin. A member of the Mormon militia, Hamblin was sent to kill Goshute cattle thieves in 1852—but had an epiphany instead: "The Holy Spirit forcibly impressed me that it was not my calling to shed the blood of the [American Indians], but to be a messenger of peace to them." Hamblin adopted a Goshute boy and began spending time with the tribe.

In 1854 Brigham Young sent Hamblin to southern Utah as an Indian missionary. Settling in Santa Clara, near present-day St. George, Hamblin embraced his calling, learning multiple languages and immersing himself in native culture. Over the next decade he cultivated relationships with the Southern Paiute, Navajo and Hopi. Hamblin ultimately won the trust of native tribes, earning him the nickname the "Buckskin Apostle." Hamblin's reputation brought him to the attention of famed explorer John Wesley Powell, who enlisted him as an interpreter and advisor on his second Colorado River expedition in 1870. According to Powell, Hamblin "speaks their language well and has great influence over the Indians in the region round about. He is a silent, reserved man, and when he speaks it is in a slow, quiet way that inspires great awe." Against long odds, Hamblin negotiated multiple peace treaties between Mormons and native tribes.

Hamblin has long been celebrated as a brave, rugged, compassionate frontiersman. While the legend obscures many personal faults, Hamblin was a rare voice of moderation in the West. Without his skills and dedication, far more blood would have been shed. Today Hamblin's pioneer-era home is open to the public as a museum in Santa Clara.

DISCOVERING ZION

In 1870, Mormon leader Brigham Young visited Springdale for the first time. Local settlers told him of a gorgeous canyon upstream they called "Zion." Young wanted to see the natural wonder firsthand, so he journeyed up the Virgin River. Exhausted by the rugged trip, he took one look around the canyon and declared that "it was not Zion"—then trudged back to Springdale. Following Young's visit, some Mormons began dutifully calling the canyon "Not Zion."

Despite the lack of local enthusiasm, Zion Canyon was starting to attract outsiders. In 1872 John Wesley Powell, fresh from his second Colorado River expedition through Grand Canyon, visited Zion with a group of scientists and artists. Powell was far more impressed than Young, though his descriptions were fairly stoic: "The walls have smooth, plain faces, and are everywhere very regular and vertical for a thousand feet or more ... everywhere as we go along, we find springs bursting out at the foot of the walls." Powell spoke with the Southern Paiute and noted that "the Indians call the cañon ... Mu-koon-tu-weap, or Straight Cañon."

Powell's geographer, Clarence Dutton (p.64), was far more exuberant. Recounting the visit years later he wrote: "In an instant, there flashed before us a scene never to be forgotten. In coming time it will, I believe, take rank with a very small number of spectacles each of which will, in its own way, be regarded as the most exquisite of its kind which the world discloses ... There is an eloquence to their forms which stirs the imagination with a singular power, and kindles in the mind of the dullest observer a glowing response."

Artists in Zion

Thomas Moran

One of the great painters of the West, Thomas Moran created monumental landscapes of the American wilderness that captivated 19th century audiences. Born in England in 1837, Moran moved with his family to Philadelphia as a boy and painted the Great Lakes as a teenager. In 1871 he was invited to join a government expedition to Yellowstone. His paintings of erupting geysers astonished East Coast audiences—who never imagined such scenery in America—and helped rally support for America's first national park. Two years later, John Wesley Powell invited Moran to explore the Colorado Plateau. "Southern Utah," wrote Moran, "is where Nature reveals herself in all her tumultuous and awe-inspiring grandeur ... for glory of scenery and stupendous scenic effects [Zion Canyon] cannot be surpassed." Moran's 1876 painting "Valley of Babbling Waters, Southern Utah" (above) was the first depiction of Zion to reach a wide audience. Moran became a leading figure of the Hudson River School, a group of artists who portrayed American landscapes as sublime manifestations of God. As Moran's daughter Ruth recalled: "To him it was all grandeur, beauty, color and light—nothing of man at all but nature, virgin, unspoiled and lovely."

Frederick Dellenbaugh

Considered Zion's most important artist, Frederick Dellenbaugh helped rally public support for protection of the park. Born in Ohio in 1853, Dellenbaugh became obsessed with the American West. In 1871, at age 17, he joined John Wesley Powell's second expedition down the Colorado River as an artist. Following the voyage Dellenbaugh passed through southern Utah, and from a distance he spotted the cliffs of Zion. "A constant desire remained with me," he wrote, "to explore this splendid region." In 1903 he returned to capture Zion's beauty on canvas, remarking that "not even the best part of Grand Canyon offers a more varied spectacle." His paintings debuted at the 1904 World's Fair in St. Louis, which drew 20 million people—roughly one-quarter of America's population at the time. Viewers flocked to Dellenbaugh's paintings but questioned whether the colorful cliffs were real. (A visitor from Utah admiring the canvases confirmed that, *yes*, Zion did actually look like that.) Dellenbaugh also penned an article titled "A New Valley of Wonders" for *Scribner's Monthly*. "The spectator," he wrote, "is instantly enveloped in the maze of cliffs and color, a double line of majestic sculptures—domes, pyramids, pinnacles, temples, sweeping away to the north, dazzling with vermillion, orange, pink, and white—all scintillating in the burning sunlight." Frederick Dellenbaugh's writings and paintings sparked public fascination with Zion, and they helped convince President William Howard Taft to declare it a national monument in 1909.

A SANCTUARY PROTECTED

By the end of the 19th century, Utah had evolved from a rogue theocracy to America's 45th state. In 1890, the Mormon church officially repudiated "celestial marriage" (polygamy), for which Utah had been repeatedly denied statehood. In 1896, Congress declared Utah a state.

A dozen years later, Leo A. Snow surveyed Zion Canyon for the U.S. government. "A view can be had of this canyon surpassed only by a similar view of the Grand Canyon of the Colorado," he wrote. "In my opinion this canyon should be set apart by the government as a national park."

On July 31, 1909, President William Howard Taft used the Antiquities Act to designate Mukuntuweap National Monument, which included Zion Canyon. But the closest train station to Mukuntuweap was in Lund, nearly 100 miles away over terrible roads. Nearby towns, eager to lure tourists, contributed funds to improve the road from La Verkin to Springdale. Utah Senator Reed Smoot secured federal funding for a road into Zion Canyon, which opened in 1917.

Railroads were also eager to benefit from tourism, so they enlisted William Wylie to build a rustic tent camp in Zion Canyon. Wylie had previously opened a tent camp in Yellowstone, which catered to middle-class families rather than well-heeled visitors looking for a deluxe lodge. He called his approach the "Wylie Way," and in Zion he charged $1 per night and $1 for meals. A package deal for two nights, including transportation from Lund, cost $26.50.

Senator Smoot

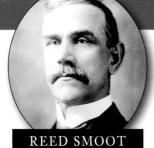

REED SMOOT

Today Utah Senator Reed Smoot is remembered not so fondly as the co-sponsor of 1930's Smoot-Hawley Tariff Act, which deepened the Great Depression. But for most of his career Smoot was famous as a tireless defender of public lands and national parks. In 1902, as a high-ranking member of the Mormon church, Smoot urged the federal government to protect all public lands in Utah watersheds. As owner of both a lumber and a sheep company, Smoot knew firsthand how unregulated business could damage the environment. The following year Smoot was elected to the U.S. Senate. He befriended fellow Republican Teddy Roosevelt, became chair of the Public Lands Committee, and joined forces with John Muir to oppose Hetch Hetchy Dam in Yosemite. Most significantly, he drafted legislation that led to the creation of the National Park Service (1916), Zion National Park (1919), and Bryce Canyon National Park (1928). Although Smoot lost reelection in 1932, his environmental legacy continues to shape both Utah and America.

In 1917 National Park Service Director Horace Albright visited Mukuntuweap. After "bouncing and crashing over some of the worst roads I had ever experienced," Albright was "overwhelmed by the loveliness of the valley and the beauty of the canyon walls and was sure that the area was of national park caliber."

Albright excitedly wired Stephen Mather, the incoming director of the National Park Service, and gushed about the scenery. Mather had never heard of Mukuntuweap, and he wondered if Albright had been given "some very potent drink." But when Mather eventually visited he was equally impressed by the landscape. (Mather was far less impressed by the roads, and he personally donated $5,000 dollars to improve them.)

When Albright returned to Washington D.C. he proposed changing the national monument's name. "I always preferred local names, especially native Indian ones," he wrote, "but 'Mukuntuweap' was too difficult to pronounce and really tough to spell." And so, on March 18, 1918, President Woodrow Wilson changed the name to Zion National Monument.

In May 1919, Senator Smoot introduced legislation to make Zion a national park, which was signed by President Wilson on November 19, 1919. Zion became America's 16th national park, and the first national park in Utah. The following September, Stephen Mather addressed an 800-person crowd at the park's formal dedication: "Today is the christening day of a most wondrous child born of God and nature—a child of such ethereal beauty that man stands enthralled in her presence ... to keep and cherish thee forever as one of the beauteous things of the earth and to christen thee—Zion National Park."

Cable Mountain

When settlers first arrived in Springdale and Rockville in the mid-1800s, they faced a severe lumber shortage. Cottonwood trees, which grow along the banks of the Virgin River, are limited and brittle. The surrounding desert supports little more than shrubs. Yet thousands of feet above, on top of Zion's sheer cliffs, are vast forests of enormous ponderosa pines.

Unfortunately, it took a full week of wagon travel over bumpy dirt roads to reach those forests, then another week of travel to haul the lumber down. At one point frustrated citizens tried tossing ponderosa logs over the rim, but the logs shattered upon impact.

Thirty miles west of Springdale, the towns of St. George and Kanab used a cable-and-pulley system to transport mail across the Vermillion Cliffs. The ingenious system saved mail carriers a full day of overland travel. One day, while contemplating the mail delivery cable, a Springdale teenager named David Flanigan had an idea. What if a more robust cable-and-pully system could transport lumber from Zion's rim?

Ten years later, when Flanigan needed lumber for his own house, he pitched the idea to fellow citizens. No one believed it was possible. Undeterred, Flanigan bought 700 pounds of bailing wire, hauled it to a 2,000-foot cliff near Weeping Rock, and spent more than two years tinkering with wires, pulleys and brakes. When it came time to test the system in 1901, he put his dog Darkey in a basket attached to the cable. Darkey rose 2,000 feet from the floor of Zion Canyon to the top of the cliff. The trip was a success, but according to later reports: "It was a week before the dog recovered fully, and since that time the vicinity of the Wire is a place he never visits."

Once the cable system was operational, Flanigan established a sawmill on the forested plateau at Stave Spring. At one point the mill employed 45 men, who sawed pines into lumber for easier transport down "The Wire." The men commuted to work in a basket attached to the cable, which rose from the floor to the rim in under three minutes.

The original cable transported more than one thousand feet of lumber per hour. In 1907, a larger cable was installed to carry even greater loads. But all that metal perched on a cliff in Canyon Country had a serious drawback. In 1908, lightning struck near the cableworks, killing two boys. A few years later the cableworks suffered a direct lightning strike, and the cable fell to the ground. Within a year, however, it was back up and running.

By the time the cableworks closed in 1926, it had transported several million feet of lumber from the rim. Its final job was hauling 240,000 feet of lumber to build Zion Lodge. Today you can visit the remains of the decaying cableworks on top of Cable Mountain (p.232).

ZION'S FIRST TOURISTS

The same day Zion became a national park it closed for the winter. Six months later, on May 15, 1920, six college girls strolled through the entrance gate on opening day. They were Zion National Park's first official visitors, but they were no ordinary tourists. The six lovely ladies had been hand-picked by the Union Pacific Railroad to promote the new park.

These "university maids"—all but one from the University of Utah—spent the previous week exploring Zion Canyon. (Although the park was officially closed during that time, a special exception was made for the ladies.) A PR man from Union Pacific choreographed their adventures. The young women carried coils of rope, climbed steep cliffs, and visited ancient archaeological sites—always with a photographer in tow.

When not commenting on the "beauty" and "splendor" of Zion, the ladies proved their Western bona fides. At one point, a guide attempted to show the girls how to properly ford the Virgin River, which was swollen with spring snowmelt. The guide fell into the river, but one of the girls, Nell Creer, who had grown up on a cattle ranch, lassoed the "mere man" and hauled him out. Another young lady, Anna Widstoe, noted that "I helped kill and then skinned two rattle snakes and brought [the] skins with me."

The media couldn't resist. *The New York Times* ran a photo of Dora Montague, "An Artist, Fair and Daring," sketching while "Suspended Over a Chasm

Hundreds of Feet Deep." Eyre Powell, writing in the *New York Tribune,* recounted the adventures of the "exploresses" who "officially opened [Zion's] first year as one of America's greatest national parks ... But more important, especially to the feminine reader, they established firmly the 1920s styles in outing togs for thousands of women who will spend the summer in the great outdoors."

In 1919, before Zion officially became a national park, 1,814 people visited. The next year, following the publicity blitz, the number more than doubled. But getting to the remote park remained a challenge. In 1923, the Union Pacific Railroad opened a spur line to Cedar Breaks, which cut driving time to Zion to three hours.

One of the first passengers on the new spur line was President Warren Harding, who became the first U.S. president to visit Zion National Park. After spending a June afternoon touring Zion Canyon on horseback Harding remarked, "I have today viewed the greatest creations of the Almighty in the majestic natural wonders of Zion National Park."

Zion Lodge opened two years later, offering the first upscale accommodations in the park. The lodge was a collaboration between the Utah Parks Company (a subsidiary of Union Pacific Railroad) and Stephen Mather, director of the National Park Service. Mather worried the fledgling park service—still less than a decade old—would survive only if people visited the parks. But his budget was limited. By collaborating with railroads, which profited from travel to remote areas, Mather dramatically boosted park visitation.

The year 1930 marked the opening of the Zion Tunnel (p.220), which permitted exploration of East Zion and dramatically cut travel time to Bryce Canyon. Union Pacific offered a package tour of the "Grand Circle," with overnight stops at Cedar Breaks, Zion, Bryce Canyon, and Grand Canyon's North Rim. The trip, which lasted eight days, cost $140 per person. Tour buses featured convertible tops so riders could better enjoy the scenery.

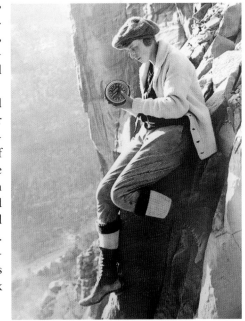

In 1930, 55,000 people visited Zion—a 30-fold increase in just over a decade. Zion's sudden popularity forever changed the character of towns just outside the park. More visitors led to better roads, which meant residents of Springdale and Rockville could visit Hurricane and St. George in hours instead of days. The era of agricultural self-sufficiency was coming to an end. In its place a more profitable industry took root: tourism.

ZION TODAY

In 1937, Kolob Canyons (p.273), located just northwest of Zion Canyon, was declared a national monument. Two decades later it became part of Zion National Park, bringing the park's total area to 229 square miles. That same year, 1956, Zion welcomed 421,000 visitors—nearly double the number from a decade earlier. People came for the scenery and the hiking, but two new outdoor sports were on the cusp of revolutionizing the landscape.

In the 1950s and 60s rock climbers, equipped with modern gear, began climbing Yosemite Valley's famous granite cliffs. After honing their skills in California, climbers spread out in search of new "big walls," which inevitably led them to Zion. The park's hardest climbs were attempted over multiple days, with climbers camping on portable ledges attached to sandstone cliffs.

Zion is also filled with fantastic slot canyons, and in the 1970s some rock climbers started using their gear to go down instead of up. Rappelling over ledges and waterfalls, they discovered natural, serpentine cathedrals sculpted from Navajo Sandstone. Before long southern Utah was ground zero for an entirely new sport: canyoneering (p.23).

Hikers were also becoming more adventurous. In 1954, Lewis F. Clark wrote an article for *National Geographic* about hiking the entire length of the Narrows. "In places we felt as if the very walls were closing in on us," Clark wrote, marveling at the "sculptured cliffs with hues of buff, red, orange, and amethyst." At the time, few people had hiked the Narrows from end to end. In the decades to come, it would become one of the park's most popular hikes.

At the time Clark's article appeared, roughly 75 percent of visitors drove to Zion in their own car. This was a huge shift from the 1920s, when most visitors arrived by train and bus. American car culture, enabled by the interstate highway system, dealt a crippling blow to railroad tourism. Throughout the 1960s the Utah Parks Company lost money, and in 1972 it donated all of its facilities, including Zion Lodge, to the park.

Car culture was liberating, but the influx of automobiles created problems that early park planners never anticipated. In 1973, over one million people visited Zion for the first time, and nearly all of them arrived by car. But Zion Canyon has just 450 parking spaces. Traffic jams, air pollution, and fights over parking spaces began to arise. By 1990, when annual park visitation topped two million, the status quo was no longer sustainable.

In the mid-1990s, the park proposed a new transportation system centered around a free shuttle in Zion Canyon. The shuttle would operate in peak season, and when it was running no private vehicles would be allowed in Zion Canyon. Free shuttles would also run through downtown Springdale, which would reduce the need for a massive parking lot in the park and keep tourist dollars flowing to local businesses.

In 2000, the Zion Shuttle debuted Memorial Day Weekend. The shuttles, which departed from a new eco-friendly visitor center (p.132), ran on clean-burning propane, which reduced air pollution. Car engines and horns no longer echoed through Zion Canyon, reducing noise pollution as well. Uncrowded roads also meant safer conditions for bicyclists and pedestrians. Zion was the first national park in the continental U.S. to implement a mandatory shuttle system, and it quickly became a model for other parks.

Those who initially opposed the shuttle worried it would lead to a drop in tourism. Over the next decade, park visitation grew nearly 10 percent. Then, following the 2013 launch of Utah's "Mighty 5" advertising campaign (which promoted the state's five national parks), visitation skyrocketed. Three million people came to Zion in 2014. Two years later, four million arrived. In 2017, over 4.5 million people visited Zion, making it America's third most popular national park (after Grand Canyon and Great Smoky Mountains).

Today Zion faces another congestion crisis. During peak season the road in Zion Canyon may be free of cars, but popular day hikes like Angels Landing and The Narrows suffer their own traffic jams. Permits, long required for overnight backpacks, might soon be required for popular day hikes.

In 1954, with scenic tourism firmly established in southern Utah, local historian Juanita Brooks wrote of the rugged landscape: "It is interesting to note that the very liabilities of the early settlers are the greatest assets of their descendants." In an era of mass tourism, whether those beautiful physical assets again become liabilities depends on the current path forward.

ZION CANYON

ZION CANYON IS the crown jewel of Zion National Park. Just nine miles long and less than 1,000 feet wide in places, this magnificent quirk of geology humbles all who enter. Luminous sandstone cliffs soar thousands of feet. Narrow slot canyons slice between peaks. Waterfalls and springs nourish lush oases. Flowing through the heart of the canyon is the Virgin River—a deceptively gentle beauty whose occasional fits of rage sculpted the astonishing scenery.

Ever since humans set foot in the canyon, they've marveled at its contours. The Southern Paiute call it *Mukuntuweap* ("Straight Up Land"). Mormon settlers declared it Zion ("Sanctuary" or "Heavenly Place"). Even today, with the frenzied modern world increasingly distracting from the natural one, the world's tallest sandstone cliffs leave many visitors speechless.

Some people come simply to marvel at the scenery, but there's no shortage of outdoor adventures. Nearly a dozen hiking trails lead to hidden alcoves and sweeping viewpoints. The Narrows (p.169) and Angels Landing (p.174) are Zion Canyon's most famous and popular hikes, but it's worth seeking out some of the less famous trails, including Observation Point (p.204) and Hidden Canyon (p.208). Easier trails include Riverside Walk (p.169), The Watchman Trail (p.172), Emerald Pools (p.150) and the Pa'rus Trail (p.134). Bicyclists enjoy uncrowded roads the length of the canyon, rock climbers defy gravity on sheer cliffs, and canyoneers rappel down fabulous, serpentine slot canyons.

If there's a downside, it's congestion—particularly in summer. Traffic jams and parking hassles led to the introduction of mandatory shuttles in 2000. For much of the year Zion Canyon is now closed to private vehicles, and visitors ride free shuttles between nine popular stops. Although shuttle lines can grow long, with a few simple tips (p.31) you can avoid the crowds and dramatically improve the quality of your visit.

An even better option is visiting in the off-season. In late October dazzling foliage lights up Zion Canyon. Winter snow falls on a peaceful canyon. Spring snowmelt activates temporary waterfalls, sets wildflowers abloom, and opens up the rims to hiking and backpacking. No matter when you visit, however, Zion Canyon is always worth it.

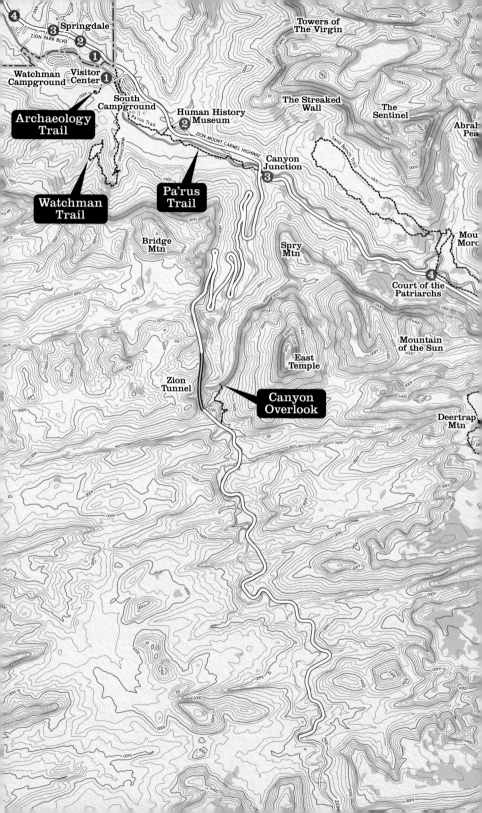

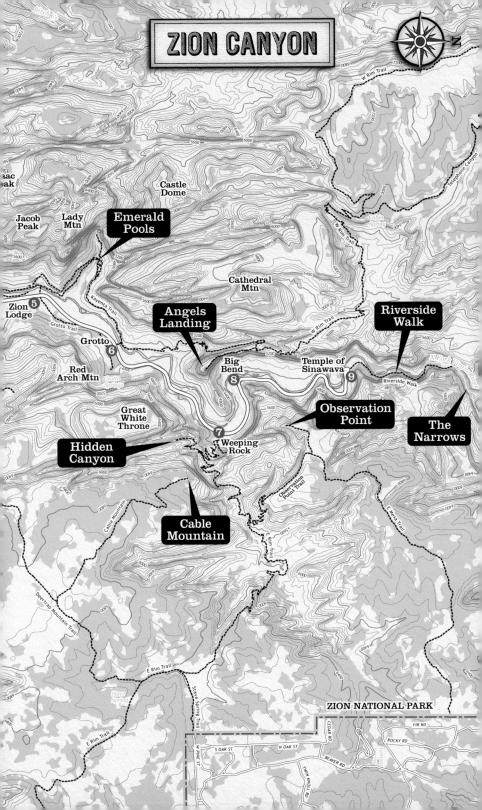

The Watchman

This majestic rock formation stands guard over Zion Canyon's south entrance. Towering 6,545 feet above sea level (2,600 feet above Springdale), the Watchman boasts over a dozen rock climbing routes. At night you can sometimes see the headlamps of rock climbers camping on The Watchman's cliffs.

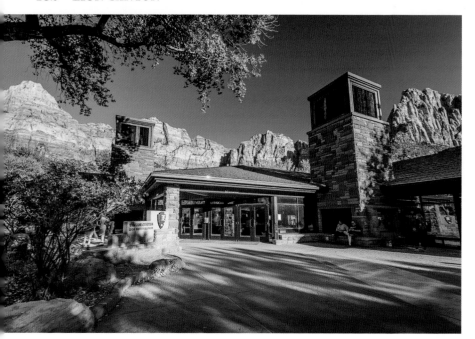

Zion Canyon Visitor Center

Located just past Zion's South Entrance Station, this is the largest visitor center in the park. If you're arriving from Springdale, the Zion Canyon Visitor Center should be your first stop. Be aware that, during peak season, the adjacent parking lot often fills by 9 a.m. If there are no parking spaces, park in Springdale (p.32) and walk through the park's pedestrian entrance located just west of the visitor center. For much of the year, Zion Canyon's free shuttle (p.14) starts and ends its round-trip loop at the visitor center.

Outdoor patios feature exhibits with basic park info. Rangers can answer more specific questions at the Visitor Information Desk inside. The main building is also home to the wilderness desk, which issues hiking, backpacking and canyoneering permits (p.14), and a large bookstore/gift shop run by The Zion Forever Project, the nonprofit partner of Zion National Park (p.39).

The Zion Canyon Visitor Center opened in 2000, and it's a marvel of green design. Twin cooling towers provide natural air conditioning through evaporation. As dry air flows over moist pads near the top of the towers, evaporation cools the air, which drops into the visitor center. In summer, the roof deflects high-angle sunlight. In winter, low-angle sunlight strikes walls and windows to generate warmth. Large, insulated windows provide natural illumination, solar panels generate electricity, light-colored pavement absorbs less heat, and native landscaping requires minimal water. The Zion Visitor Center cost 30% less to build than comparable visitor centers, and it reduced energy use by over 70%.

Archeology Trail

This short, 0.2-mile trail rises 80 feet above the north end of Watchman Campground to the remains of an Ancestral Puebloan archaeological site that was occupied between AD 700 and 950. Perched high above the flood level of the Virgin River, it may have been used to store and prepare food. Over 1,600 artifacts have been uncovered here, including stone tools and ceramics now on display at the Zion Human History Museum (p.137). After archaeologists excavated the site they filled it in for protection. Today just a few stone foundations remain. Although some people find the "ruins" underwhelming, it's fun to visit at sunset, gaze across the canyon, and imagine what human life was like here over 1,000 years ago.

Pa'rus Trail

Stretching 1.8 miles from South Campground (near the Zion Canyon Visitor Center) to Canyon Junction (p.142), the Pa'rus Trail parallels a lovely stretch of the Virgin River. Four small bridges cross the river, and a handful of side trails descend to the water. *Pa'rus* (pronounced *PA-roos*) is a Paiute word that means "white foaming water." The paved path— the only trail open to bikes and pets on leashes in Zion—is an easy walk that's good for strollers and wheelchairs. Abundant vegetation makes the Pa'rus Trail great for birdwatching. Free "What's Flyin' in Zion" ranger walks are sometimes offered on the trail (inquire at the visitor center).

Zion Nature Center

Located just north of South Campground, the Zion Nature Center is oriented towards kids, but it's a terrific destination for anyone interested in wildlife. Natural history exhibits offer fascinating facts about the birds, mammals and reptiles that call Zion home. Exhibits range from old-school taxidermy in glass cases to a life-size replica of a California condor hanging from the ceiling. There are also books, games and puzzles. Children ages 6 to 12 can participate in Junior Ranger activities from Memorial Day through Labor Day. The Zion Nature Center is open 2 p.m. to 6 p.m. daily in summer.

One of the oldest buildings in Zion, the Zion Nature Center was designed by Gilbert Stanley Underwood, architect of Zion Lodge (p.148). It's a classic example of National Park Service rustic style, which uses native materials to blend

in seemlessly with the natural scenery. When it opened in 1934, the building was used as the office and cafeteria of the Zion Inn, which offered overnight accommodation in surrounding cabins. In 1972 the Zion Inn closed, the cabins were sold, and the cafeteria was transformed into a nature center. In 1987 the Zion Nature Center was listed on the National Register of Historic Places.

Zion Human History Museum

One mile past Zion's South Entrance Station is the Zion Human History Museum (shuttle stop #2). Inside you'll find artifacts related to the human history of Zion, from prehistoric tribes to early Mormon settlers. There's also a bookstore, gift shop, and small theater that shows the free Zion movie "Where Forever is Now." Ranger programs are offered throughout the day on the back patio. Even if there's no ranger program when you visit, it's worth checking out the back patio to enjoy the fabulous views of the Towers of the Virgin (p.138), a line of imposing cliffs towering above Oak Creek Canyon.

In the late 1800s, a small community of Mormon pioneers lived in Oak Creek Canyon, including the Crawford family, who owned 360 acres where the museum now stands. Oak Creek provided irrigation for vegetable gardens, orchards and hay fields. A small pond provided ice in the winter. Dairy cows provided fresh milk year-round. But farm life was challenging, and in the 1930s the Crawford family sold its property to the National Park Service.

The Human History Museum, which opened as a visitor center in 1960, was part of the Mission 66 Project to modernize national parks by 1966—the 50th anniversary of the National Park Service. Following World War II, visitation to national parks soared as new highways opened up vast stretches of America to anyone with a car. The Human History Museum is a classic example of the "modern" style popular in the 1960s, which rejected rustic ornamentation in favor of simple, geometric lines.

West Temple
(7,810 feet)

Sundial
(7,590 feet)

Towers of the Virgin

Behind the Human History Museum the Towers of the Virgin rise 4,000 feet above Oak Creek Canyon. West Temple, which tops out at 7,810 feet, is the tallest point in Zion Canyon. In 1903 artist Frederick Dellenbaugh wrote: "Never before has such a naked mountain of rock entered into our minds ... we are at last face to face with the Unattainable; no foot of man has ever touched the summit of this silent shrine." Three decades later, brothers Newell and Norman Crawford reached West Temple's summit. The Sundial earned its name because residents of Grafton once set their clocks to shadows cast by the peak. The Altar of Sacrifice is named for the "blood stains" dripping down its Navajo Sandstone sides. The red stains are actually hematite (iron oxide) washed down from the iron-rich Temple Cap Formation, which sits atop the Navajo Sandstone.

Altar of
Sacrifice
(7,505 feet)

Crawford Arch

From the front patio of the Human History Museum, gaze across the canyon to Bridge Mountain. About halfway up, barely visible to the naked eye, is one of the most impressive rock arches in Zion. Named after the Crawford family, which settled here in the late 1800s, Crawford Arch measures 3 feet wide by 156 feet long. Although it's possible to hike to Crawford Arch, the strenuous trek takes upwards of 16 hours and requires rappelling and rock climbing.

Canyon Junction

Shuttle stop #3 marks the junction of Zion's two most popular destinations. To the north lie the wonders of Zion Canyon. To the east the Zion-Mt. Carmel Highway twists up Pine Creek Canyon to East Zion's slickrock dreamscape (p.215). Canyon Junction is also the northern terminus of the Pa'rus Trail (p.134). But many tripod-wielding visitors arrive here with a single purpose: sunset photos from Canyon Junction Bridge. In the foreground, the quicksilver Virgin River. In the background, The Watchman illuminated by the setting sun. Visit in late October and cottonwoods shimmer with gold. As sunset approaches, the bridge often fills to capacity. Tip: enjoy sunset along the Pa'rus Trail, which has similar views with a fraction of the crowds.

Canyon Junction

Sentinel Slide

Court of the Patriarchs

Sentinel Slide

Just north of Canyon Junction, a giant debris pile slopes above the Virgin River's west bank. Called Sentinel Slide, it's the remnant of a massive "rock avalanche" that occurred 4,800 years ago when one of the surrounding cliffs collapsed. In just 20 seconds, *ten billion* cubic feet of rock came crashing down. The resulting debris pile, which measured two miles long by nearly a mile wide, dammed the river and created a lake that stretched more than five miles upstream (p.60). Seven hundred years later, the Virgin River broke through the dam and drained the lake. Although the Virgin River has removed much of the debris over the past 4,000 years, more than half of the rock avalanche remains, and "mini-landslides" occasionally block the river. In April 1995, the Virgin undercut a portion of Sentinel Slide, triggering a landslide that rerouted the river and washed out 200 yards of road. Hundreds of guests were stranded at the Zion Lodge until the road was repaired. As erosion continues, future landslides are inevitable. If you'd like to explore Sentinel Slide, the Sand Bench Trail (accessible from Court of the Patriarchs) makes a 3.4-mile loop around the top of the debris.

1995 Landslide

Court of the Patriarchs

Shuttle stop #4 offers great views of three dramatic peaks known as the Three Patriarchs. The name was given by Claude Hirschi, who visited Zion in 1916 with Methodist minister Frederick Vining Fisher. As he gazed upon the peaks, Hirschi was reminded of the Old Testament patriarchs Abraham, Isaac and Jacob. A fourth peak, Mount Moroni, was named after the angel who presented Joseph Smith with the golden plates from which he translated the Book of Mormon. Although Mount Moroni is over 1,000 feet shorter than any of the Three Patriarchs, from the shuttle stop it appears nearly as high because it's physically closer.

Isaac
(6,825 feet)

Abraham
(6,890 feet)

Behind the shuttle stop a paved 50-yard path heads to a nice viewpoint of the Three Patriarchs. But there are better views across the street. Follow Service Road past the horse stables—used for horse rides on Sand Bench (p.145)—and continue over the bridge until you reach a T-intersection. If an uncrowded trail above the Virgin River seems nicer than a crowded shuttle, turn right and follow Emerald Pools Trail one mile to Zion Lodge (shuttle stop #5).

If you'd like to challenge the Patriarchy, three popular rock climbing routes head up Isaac, whose cliffs rise 1,600 feet above the floor of Birch Creek Canyon. The first ascent was in 1972 along a route dubbed "Freeloader." The other routes are called "Tricks of the Trade" and "Iron Like A Lion in Zion."

Mount Moroni
(5,690 feet)

Jacob
(6,831 feet)

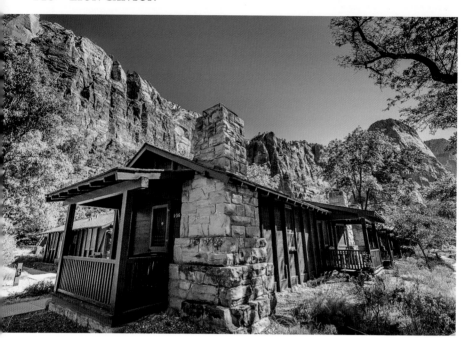

Zion Lodge

This historic lodge (shuttle stop #5) offers Zion Canyon's only overnight accommodations. Forty rustic cabins cost $220 per night, and luxury suites top $275. Non-guests can enjoy the gift shop or two restaurants: the cafeteria-style Castle Dome Café or the sit-down Red Rock Grill. But the best (and cheapest) activity is enjoying the beautiful views from rocking chairs on the front porch.

Zion Lodge was designed by Gilbert Stanley Underwood, who also designed Grand Canyon Lodge and Yosemite's Ahwahnee Hotel. Underwood's original design called for a grandiose, three-story structure, but National Park Service director Stephen Mather wanted something less intrusive in Zion. So Underwood went back to the drawing board and designed a more humble central lodge surrounded by small cabins. Logs used in construction were brought down from Cable Mountain (p.120), and in 1925 Zion Lodge opened to great acclaim. Then, during a 1966 remodel gone awry, the central lodge burned to the ground. A new "modern" structure was hastily assembled in 100 days, but two decades of complaints led to restoration of the original exterior in 1990.

An enormous cottonwood towers above the front lawn in front of the lodge. The 100-foot tree, which was planted around 1929, has grown unusually large thanks to regular watering. By some estimates it consumes upwards of 1,000 gallons of water each day. To ensure its continued health, an arborist inspects the cottonwood twice annually. Cuttings from the tree, which grow in Zion's Native Plant Nursery, will someday replace the elderly cottonwood when it dies.

Emerald Pools

These lovely pools, which cascade through Heaps Canyon, are some of Zion's most popular day hikes. Lower Emerald Pool is a misty amphitheater reached via an easy, paved 0.6-mile path that starts across from Zion Lodge. Upon reaching the amphitheater, the trail wraps around curved cliffs dotted with dripping seeps and springs. Look for colorful flowers like shooting stars and golden columbine (p.72) in the spring. Delicate waterfalls trickle 50 feet from above, but during rainstorms the trickles can turn into torrents. The pools below were once tinted green by algae, but the emerald color has long since faded.

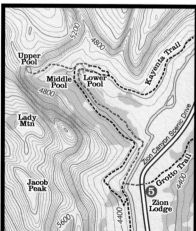

At the far end of the amphitheater the trail ascends roughly a quarter-mile to Middle Pool, which feeds the Lower Emerald Pool waterfalls. Enjoy the dramatic canyon views, but keep away from the exposed edge, which is covered with slippery algae. Several people have fallen and died here.

The half-mile trail to Upper Pool is sandy and strenuous, but the payoff is the loveliest pool of all, fed by a 400-foot waterfall surrounded by sheer cliffs. Look and listen for tree frogs (p.101), whose curious mating call sounds like sheep.

The Grotto

Located across the road from the Angels Landing trailhead (p.174), the Grotto (shuttle stop #6) lures a steady stream of ambitious hikers. Just south of the shuttle stop there's a small stone cabin. Built in 1924, it was the original Zion Canyon visitor center. Today it's the oldest surviving building in the park and the temporary home of Zion's artist in residence. In exchange for one month of free housing, artists in residence give public presentations and/or donate some of their works to the park.

In the late 1860s, Mormon polygamist John Rolf built two homes in Zion Canyon: one for his first wife at The Grotto and another for his second wife near Emerald Pools. One evening Rolf's neighbor, Isaac Behunin, gazed upon the mountains above The Grotto and recalled a passage from the Bible: "Come ye, and let us go up the mountain of the Lord ... and we will walk in his paths: for out of Zion shall go forth the law." His epiphany resonated with other settlers, who started calling the canyon Zion. The Grotto was later farmed by Oliver D. Gifford. In 1880 a giant rock slab broke free from a nearby mountain and crashed onto Gifford's property. No one was injured, but the rockfall left an enormous arch in the mountain, which became known as Red Arch Mountain.

Early settlers ultimately abandoned Zion Canyon because of its physical challenges, including limited sunlight, which made growing crops a challenge. Later, the park built its first campground at The Grotto, but the campground was eventually shut down due to rockfall risk.

"To eyes prejudiced by the soft blues and grays of a familiar Eastern United States or European district, this immense prodigality of color is startling, perhaps painful; it seems to the inflexible mind unwarranted, immodest, as if Nature had stripped and posed nude, unblushing, before humanity."

—Frederick Dellenbaugh, 1904

Lady Mountain

Located northwest of Zion Lodge, Lady Mountain is named for markings that reminded early visitors of a lady's face. In 1925 the park service opened a strenuous trail to its summit. With 1,400 stone steps, over 1,000 feet of cable, and sections requiring ladders, the Lady Mountain Trail was considered more challenging than Angels Landing. It claimed its first victim in 1930, and as accidents mounted park officials concluded the trail was too dangerous. The Lady Mountain Trail was dismantled in the 1970s, although rock climbers continue to use some sections today.

Angels Landing

When Methodist minister Frederick Vining Fisher visited Zion Canyon in 1916, he gazed upon this pinnacle and concluded that it was "so high only an angel could land on it." Ten years later, Zion National Park debuted the dramatic trail to "Angels Landing." Now considered one of America's greatest hikes, the Angels Landing Trail (p.174) is listed on the National Register of Historic Places. Over the past century, hundreds of thousands of people have stood on top of Angels Landing, which at 1,488 feet remains taller than any building west of the Mississippi.

"Up and down, east and west, extends the labyrinthian array of giant rock-forms so magnificently sculptured, so ravishingly tinted ... It is doubtful if in this respect the valley has anywhere its equal. Not even the best part of the Grand Canyon offers a more varied spectacle. There is an isolation of each temple here that is rare, yet all are welded together in a superb ensemble."

—Frederick Dellenbaugh, 1904

Weeping Rock

This popular shuttle stop (#7) offers fascinating geology, lush hanging gardens, and terrific views. From the parking area a half-mile trail climbs 100 feet to Weeping Rock, where water oozes out of Navajo Sandstone, nourishing ferns and flowers. As the trail approaches Weeping Rock, it dips behind a curtain of water. Expect to get a little wet! The trail then enters a moist overhanging alcove with mineral deposits that form dramatic zebra stripes. A small waterfall fed by Echo Canyon trickles over Weeping Rock. During rainstorms or periods of heavy runoff this trickle turns into one of Zion Canyon's most beautiful waterfalls.

The water dripping out of Weeping Rock is over 1,000 years old. Around A.D. 800 it fell as rain or snow on the Navajo Sandstone above. Because sandstone is porous and permeable, the precipitation soaked into the rock and spent the next 1,200 years percolating down. When it reached the bottom of the Navajo Sandstone, the water encountered the relatively impermeable Kayenta Formation rock layer. Unable to flow down farther, the water flowed horizontally along cracks and emerged at Weeping Rock. Scientists call this "fossil water" because it is so old. The water is rich with calcium and other minerals, which precipitate out to form a limestone rock called tufa. The striped overhang at Weeping Rock is actually a large tufa deposit.

If you're interested in some strenuous hikes with terrific views, trails to both Hidden Canyon (p.208) and Observation Point (p.204) start just past the Weeping Rock parking area.

Great White Throne

Towering 2,300 feet above the floor of Zion Canyon, the Great White Throne reaches a maxium height of 6,744 feet. Originally called El Gobernador ("The Governor" in Spanish), it was rechristened the Great White Throne in 1916 when Methodist minister Frederick Vining Fisher saw it glistening in the sun. "Never have I seen such a sight before," Fisher told his companions. "It is by all odds America's masterpiece. Boys, I have looked for this mountain all my life but never expected to find it in this world. This mountain is the Great White Throne."

The Organ

The same day Frederick Vining Fisher named the Great White Throne, his companion Claud Hirschi named the Great Organ—now called simply The Organ. Because The Organ is composed of relatively soft sedimentary rock, geologists joke that it only plays "soft rock." Someday, however, this rock might roll. Zion geologist Wayne Hamilton once called The Organ a "likely candidate" for a rock formation that could tumble into the Virgin River, creating a natural dam that would form a lake in Zion Canyon.

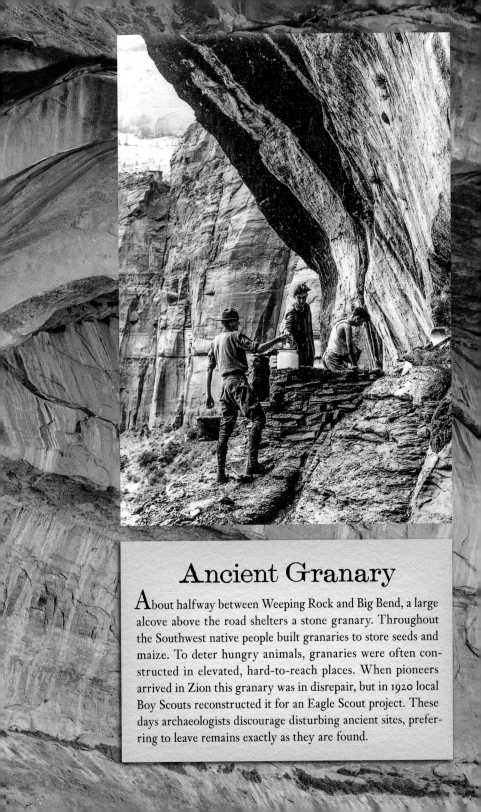

Ancient Granary

About halfway between Weeping Rock and Big Bend, a large alcove above the road shelters a stone granary. Throughout the Southwest native people built granaries to store seeds and maize. To deter hungry animals, granaries were often constructed in elevated, hard-to-reach places. When pioneers arrived in Zion this granary was in disrepair, but in 1920 local Boy Scouts reconstructed it for an Eagle Scout project. These days archaeologists discourage disturbing ancient sites, preferring to leave remains exactly as they are found.

Big Bend

At first glance, this hairpin turn seems to offer little more than ... well, a big bend in the road. But it's worth a quick stop. The skies above are one of the best places in the park to spot California condors, the largest birds in North America (p.84). Once on the verge of extinction, California condors now fly free in a handful of remote areas, including Zion. As the late morning sun heats up the canyon, condors spread their nine-foot wingspans and soar on thermal columns.

Big Bend is also a great place to spot another gravity-defying species: rock climbers. The surrounding cliffs, which are particularly sheer and easily accessible, offer some of the best climbing in the park, including multi-day routes where climbers spend the night strapped to a portable ledge. The abundance of red rocks near Big Bend also attracts climbers because red rocks have more iron than white rocks, which makes them stronger and less crumbly.

Directly across the river lies the north face of Angels Landing, which has five popular climbing routes. Another half dozen routes are located behind the shuttle stop. But the most celebrated climb is located half a mile upstream. Originally called Chimney Rock, it was rechristened Moonlight Buttress during a full moon first ascent in 1971. Then, on April 1, 2008, a 22-year-old named Alex Honnold became the first person to free solo (climb without ropes or protection) Moonlight Buttress—an accomplishment so astonishing most climbers assumed it was an April Fool's joke. It wasn't, and Honnold went on to become the world's most celebrated rock climber, star of the Oscar-winning documentary *Free Solo*.

Menu Falls

This lovely, unmarked waterfall—which earned its name because it once graced the cover of the Zion Lodge dinner menu—is located half a mile north of Big Bend. A two-tiered stairway leads to a viewing platform where you can enjoy the delicate scenery. The water at Menu Falls, which flows from Navajo Sandstone aquifers above, has been dated at over 4,000 years old!

Temple of Sinawava

This beautiful alcove is Zion Canyon's final shuttle stop (#9). It's also the start of Riverside Walk (p.169) and The Narrows (p.184), two of Zion's most popular hikes. Bathrooms and drinking water are located across from the shuttle stop. If you happen to visit during a rainstorm, the Temple of Sinawava is a great place to see ephemeral waterfalls pouring down from the surrounding cliffs. Riverside Walk is a paved path that starts just past the shuttle stop and continues one mile to the entrance of The Narrows. Even if you don't feel like walking the entire path, it's worth hiking a short distance and exploring the gorgeous banks of the Virgin River.

Rising above a dramatic horseshoe bend in the Virgin River is a large rock spire called the Pulpit. Zion's first Euro-American visitors believed the canyon was proof of God's magnificence. As Mormon pioneer Isaac Behunin put it: "A man can worship god among these great cathedrals as well as in any man-made church." In 1913 Douglas White, a Union Pacific Railroad publicist, came up with the name "Temple of Sinawava" to pay homage to the Southern Paiute's friendly, benevolent wolf-god. (Although wolves were once present in Zion, they were hunted out of the region by the 1930s.) The Southern Paiute believed their temperamental trickster god, Kinesava, hid in Zion Canyon's shadows. Early settlers reported that the Southern Paiute refused to enter Zion Canyon after sundown, but according to a Paiute Elder in 2009: "You would be afraid to go into the canyon too with some crazy white man shooting at you."

Riverside Walk

This easy, one-mile paved trail heads from the Temple of Sinawava to the start of The Narrows (p.184). Paralleling the Virgin River, it's a gorgeous introduction to the visual drama of The Narrows without having to get wet. Along the way you'll pass multiple springs and hanging gardens. Keep your eyes out for the elusive Zion snail (p.101), which is only found in Zion. The further you walk, the narrower the canyon becomes, until eventually you reach the entrance to The Narrows. When flash floods are likely, the park closes Riverside Walk.

"The tiny oases huddle in their pockets in the rock, surrounded on all sides by as terrible and beautiful wasteland as the world can show, colored every color of the spectrum even to blue and green, sculptured by sandblast winds, fretted by meandering lines of cliffs hundreds of miles long and often several thousand feet high, carved and broken and split by canyons so deep and narrow that the rivers run in sunless depths and cannot be approached for miles."

—Wallace Stegner

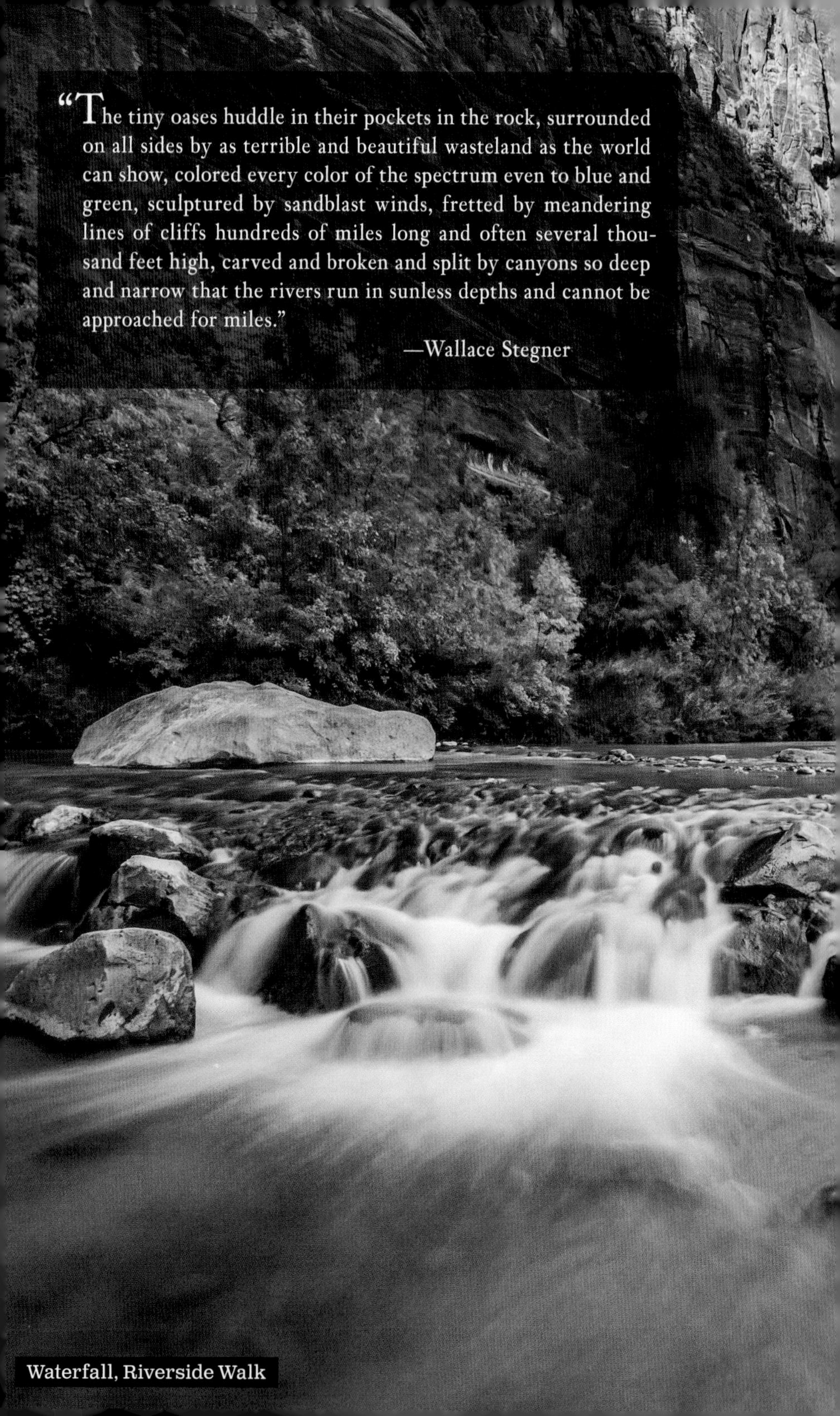

Waterfall, Riverside Walk

⚘ WATCHMAN TRAIL ⤳

SUMMARY Rising to the top of a small plateau just south of the visitor center, the Watchman Trail offers panoramic views without too much effort, making it one of the best family hikes in the park. (Tip: If the morning shuttle line is long, consider hiking the Watchman Trail while the line shortens.) The trail climbs switchbacks carved into soft Moenave Formation rocks, then makes a 0.3-mile loop around the top, passing a number of great viewpoints. To the south, the jagged peak of The Watchman (above) towers over Springdale. To the west, a wall of sheer cliffs marches north into the heart of Zion Canyon. Running through the center of the canyon is a green strip of vegetation watered by the Virgin River. As you gaze over the widest part of Zion Canyon, you'll enjoy nearly complete views of Zion's rock layers—from Moenkopi to Temple Cap (p.50). Tip: Avoid hiking in the early afternoon, when temperatures peak on the sunny trail.

TRAILHEAD The trail starts just north of the Zion Canyon Visitor Center, follows the banks of the Virgin River before crossing the Service Road and climbing up the hill.

TRAIL INFO

RATING: Moderate

HIKING TIME: 1.5–2 hours

DISTANCE: 3.3 miles round-trip

ELEVATION CHANGE: 368 feet

❧ ANGELS LANDING ❧

SUMMARY Angels Landing is one of the most iconic hikes in America—and with good reason. The trail to the seemingly inaccessible summit passes along a thin, rocky ridge with 1,000-foot dropoffs on either side. Only thick metal chains bolted into the rock offer protection in the form of handholds. Though not technically challenging, Angels Landing is not for those with a fear of heights. Be aware that over a dozen people have died on the trail. Also be aware that hundreds of thousands more have lived—and experienced views they will never forget. Standing on the summit of Angels Landing, surrounded by extraordinary panoramas in the heart of Zion Canyon, is nothing short of sublime. If you've got the mental and physical stamina to conquer this 1,500-foot altar, Angels Landing will leave you in a state of rapture.

TRAILHEAD The trail to Angels Landing starts near The Grotto shuttle stop (#6). Tip: Use the bathrooms at The Grotto; the toilets at Scout Lookout are overwhelmed. From the shuttle stop, cross the road and walk across the footbridge over the Virgin River. Turn right and follow the well-trodden trail.

◆ TRAIL INFO ◆

RATING: Strenuous   **DISTANCE:** 5 miles round-trip

HIKING TIME: 4–5 hours   **ELEVATION CHANGE:** 1,488 feet

Angels Landing

Scout Lookout

Walter's Wiggles

Angels Landing Trail Description

The trail to Angels Landing starts across the street from The Grotto (shuttle stop #6). After crossing a footbridge, stroll above the west bank of the Virgin River, then ascend toward the steep cliffs looming above. As you climb higher and higher, gorgeous views of Zion Canyon unfold below. A series of switchbacks takes you to a long, straight section blasted into the side of Cathedral Mountain. Although the dropoff is steep, the trail is fairly wide and rocks provide a small barrier on the edge. After rounding a corner you'll head into Refrigerator Canyon.

REFRIGERATOR CANYON (1.3 MILES) Carved deep into the cliffs between Cathedral Mountain and Angels Landing, Refrigerator Canyon receives little sunlight and is noticeably cooler than the rest of the trail. Take some time to enjoy the fabulous geology. Also notice the plants, many of which are normally found at higher (cooler) elevations. Particularly noteworthy are bigtooth maples, whose leaves turn bright red in autumn.

WALTER'S WIGGLES (1.8 MILES) To exit Refrigerator Canyon you'll need to climb Walter's Wiggles, a series of 21 steep switchbacks. The Wiggles aren't technically demanding, but their 19% grade is sure to quicken your pulse. The switchbacks are named after Walter Ruesch, the park's first custodian (superintendent), who helped design and build the trail in the mid-1920s.

SCOUT LOOKOUT (2.1 MILES) Beyond the top of Walter's Wiggles lies Scout Lookout, the final patch of non-scary terrain before the knife-edge route to Angels Landing begins. This is a great place to stop for a snack or lunch, but watch out for aggressive squirrels and chipmunks. The fearless rodents will nibble holes in unattended backpacks in their quest for tasty people food. Two toilets are perched above Scout Lookout—and you might need to use them after glimpsing the final stretch of trail.

THE SPINE (FINAL 0.4 MILES) This is, without question, the most intimidating section of the hike. It's also what makes Angels Landing legendary. "The construction of this trail which ascends the spine of a steep-sided sandstone cliff was unique and daring," says the National Register of Historic Places. "Angels Landing is one of the most dramatic trails ever built by the Park Service." Although the elevation gain is just 300 feet, it feels far greater. Much of this section has chains bolted into the rock to use as handholds. There are a few sections that require short climbs, plus several very exposed sections. Crowds often complicate the hike. Be respectful. Don't rush. The summit of Angels Landing, 5,790 feet above sea level, has no guardrails but there's enough space to spread out and relax on the relatively flat peak. After enjoying the gorgeous views, head back the way you came.

Angels Landing Dangers

Everyone knows falling is the number one danger on Angels Landing ... right? Wrong! Based on the number of incidents, squirrel and chipmunk bites are actually the #1 danger on Angels Landing. Most bites happen at Scout Lookout, where many hikers stop for a snack or lunch, and where local rodents are unusually aggressive. The real problem, however, is people feeding the adorable critters. Contrary to Hollywood wisdom, chipmunks won't sing and dance and take you on a fabulous adventure to meet your true love. They'll bite your hand, resulting in blood, stitches or even disease.

Of course, falling is far more consequential. But if you're cautious and act responsibly, you should be fine. Don't let your fear of falling distract you from the far more common threats of dehydration and heat stroke, both of which can lead to impaired judgement—which increases your chance of falling. Another great way to avoid falling is to skip the trail entirely when conditions are wet, icy or stormy.

Death on Angels Landing

As of this writing, a sign at the Angels Landing trailhead states that seven people have died falling from cliffs along the trail since 2004. Scary? Sure. But in the seven-year period from 2011 to 2017 nobody died, despite a surge in visitation. And prior to 2000 (aka the millennia before dramatic danger selfies), just one person died falling off the trail. It's true that Angels Landing is riskier than your average trail, but it's also worth remembering that well over 99.99% of Angels Landing hikers have lived. Always use caution, and be aware that more people die descending Angels Landing than ascending. That might be because they're tired. Another possibility is that some hikers acquire a false sense of confidence upon reaching the summit, then get reckless on the way down. Be careful when hiking and treat this magnificent trail with the respect it deserves.

Permits

In 2022, Zion National Park began requiring permits for all Angels Landing hikers. This was done to reduce congestion on the trail, which had become overwhelming. Permits are required to hike between Scout Lookout and Angels Landing, and permits are allocated through a lottery system. As of this writing, there are two lotteries: An advance Seasonal Lottery, held two months before the hiking date, and a Day-before lottery held—you guessed it—the day before the hiking date. Check Zion National Park's website (nps.gov/zion) for the most up-to-date information about Angels Landing permits.

Heading back from Angels Landing

View Southwest from Angels Landing

View Northeast from Angels Landing

⇨ NARROWS (BOTTOM-UP) ⇦

SUMMARY The Narrows is one of the most spectacular hikes in America. The "trail" is essentially the Virgin River, which twists and turns through a gorgeous slot canyon less than 20 feet wide in places. Sandstone cliffs tower thousands of feet above, catching sunlight that illuminates the otherwise dark corridor. Most of the time you'll be ankle-deep in water, but depending on the river's flow there may be some chest-deep or even swimming sections. Proper gear is essential (p.188). The Narrows stretches 16 miles from start to finish, but bottom-up hikers are restricted to Big Spring, located 3.6 miles from the trailhead. Hiking to Big Spring and back can take up to eight hours, but closer destinations—Orderville Canyon, Wall Street—are no less remarkable. Even a short hike in The Narrows is worth it. If you love bold geology, have a sense of adventure, and don't mind getting wet, The Narrows will likely be the highlight of your trip.

TRAILHEAD The Narrows hike starts at the Temple of Sinawava (shuttle stop #9), then follows Riverside Walk to the Virgin River. Tip: use the bathrooms at the Temple of Sinawava; there are no bathrooms in The Narrows.

TRAIL INFO

RATING: Strenuous

DISTANCE: Up to 7.2 miles

HIKING TIME: 1–10 hours

ELEVATION CHANGE: Up to 500 ft.

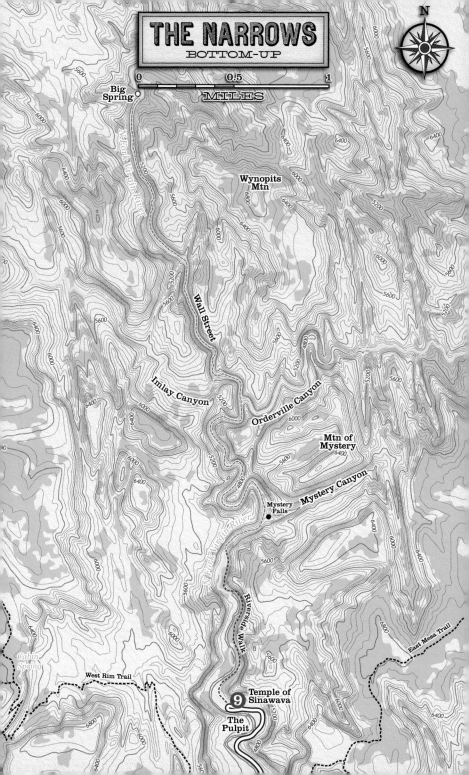

Best Times to Hike The Narrows

The best time to explore the Narrows is when the Virgin River's flow is low (which makes hiking easier) and ambient temperatures are warm (which mitigates the cold of the river and the cool, shady canyon). In spring, snowmelt generates high flows and temperatures can still be chilly. As spring turns into summer, flows reduce and temperatures warm. Many people consider June the best month to hike the Narrows. Summer has delightful temperatures, but monsoon season from July to September (p.35) creates the highest risk of deadly flash floods. Fall flows are generally low, but it can also be cold. Winter has the lowest flows, but freezing temperatures deter all but the most rugged hikers.

If you're planning on hiking all the way to Big Spring, start as early as possible to give yourself plenty of time to return before sundown. If you only plan on hiking a few hours, it's far more pleasant to start in the late morning or early afternoon when temperatures have warmed significantly.

The Virgin River's Flow

The Virgin River's flow is measured in cubic feet per second (cfs). When flows exceed 150 cfs, the park closes the Narrows for safety. Spring snowmelt often keeps the Narrows closed from March to late May. Following big snow years, the Narrows can sometimes stay closed until mid-July. The Virgin River's current flow is posted at the Zion Visitor Center and at local outfitters. Flows below 50 cfs mean relatively easy hiking, with occasional waist-deep wading. Higher flows become progressively more difficult, with chest-deep or swimming sections.

Flash Floods

Flash floods are the biggest danger in the Narrows. They can appear with little warning, creating a wall of water that cannot be outrun. Your only chance of survival is scrambling to higher ground—but the Narrows' sheer cliffs often make this impossible. The good news? There have been remarkably few flash flood fatalities in recent decades. Park officials constantly monitor the weather and close the Narrows whenever flash floods are likely. That said, flash floods are always a potential threat, so you should recognize the warning signs. See page 16 for more about flash floods in Zion.

Other Dangers

More people are rescued from the Narrows than any other place in the park, and most rescues are due to twisted ankles and broken bones—the result of hikers stumbling in swift currents or slipping on wet rocks. Proper hiking gear is essential (see following page). Also be aware that temperatures in the shady Narrows are 20–30˚F cooler than in Zion Canyon, so warm clothes are essential.

Narrows Hiking Gear

Not all of this gear is essential, but a walking staff, canyoneering shoes, and neoprene socks are highly recommended. Wear quick-drying synthetic shorts, never long pants. A waterproof bag or ziplock bag keeps food or electronics dry. You can rent or buy gear from Springdale outfitters (p.45).

WALKING STAFF

A sturdy staff helps maintain your balance when you stumble (and *everyone* stumbles in the Narrows). A thick wooden staff is better than skinny hiking poles, which can sometimes get stuck between rocks.

CANYONEERING SHOES

These rugged shoes have grippy soles and a thick protective outer layer. It's possible to use hiking boots or closed-toe water shoes, but canyoneering shoes are superior. Bestard and Adidas make excellent canyoneering shoes.

NEOPRENE SOCKS

Thick neoprene socks keep your feet warm when walking in the cold river. They also provide extra cushioning.

WETSUIT

When the Virgin River runs high, a neoprene wetsuit helps keep you warm while swimming or wading through deep sections. Slightly bulky, but worth every penny if you tend to get cold.

DRYSUIT

Drysuits are even warmer than wetsuits, but bulkier and a bit more fragile. A good choice during the coldest months (November through April). Avoid overall-style "waders" that can inadvertently fill with water and weigh you down.

The Narrows Trail Description

TRAILHEAD The Narrows starts at the Temple of Sinawava. The first mile follows Riverside Walk (p.169), a one-mile paved trail above the east bank of the Virgin River. There are no toilets in the Narrows—and very little privacy—so be sure to use the bathrooms at the Temple of Sinawava before hiking.

END OF RIVERSIDE WALK (1 MILE) This is where you step off the Riverside Walk and into the river. Brace yourself—the water is cold and the rocks are slippery. It's easy to stumble. Don't rush. Take some time to get used to the strange nature of walking in the Virgin River. After five or ten minutes you'll feel more comfortable, and you can hike upriver at a faster pace. Most hikers travel between 0.5 miles and 1 mile per hour.

MYSTERY FALLS (1.4 MILES) From the elevated mouth of Mystery Canyon a narrow ribbon of water tumbles down a cliff into the Virgin River. In the afternoon, canyoneers often rappel down the face of this cliff. These canyoneers have just finished a 10-mile scramble through Mystery Canyon, whose grand finale is descending into the Narrows in front of wide-eyed onlookers below.

ORDERVILLE CANYON (1.6 MILES) Orderville Canyon (p.192) is one of the most popular destinations for bottom-up Narrows hikers. It's just far enough to be challenging, yet not as demanding as the trek to Big Spring. You can hike 0.4 miles into Orderville Canyon before reaching Veiled Falls, a beautiful waterfall that blocks further progress.

WALL STREET Near the junction with Orderville Canyon, the Narrows passes through a particularly narrow section known as Wall Street. In places, the walls are just 20 feet apart. Exploring this roughly one-mile corridor feels like stepping into a grand, natural cathedral.

BIG SPRING (3.6 MILES) Located on the left (west) bank of the Virgin River, this gushing spring is a lush oasis of vegetation and serene waterfalls. Day hikers must turn around at this point. Take a moment to enjoy the scenery, then start the long, beautiful hike back.

Permits

As of this writing, permits are not required for bottom-up day hikers. But that could change soon because the number of Narrows hikers is becoming overwhelming in peak season. In 2018 the National Park Service held public forums about potential changes to the current system. Check the Zion National Park website (nps.gov/zion) for the most up-to-date information.

Wading through The Narrows. Zebra stripes on rock walls are the result of minerals deposited by seeping water.

Orderville Canyon Junction

Big Spring

◁ NARROWS (TOP-DOWN) ▷

SUMMARY Hiking The Narrows top-down is even better than hiking bottom-up for three reasons: 1) you can explore the entire 16-mile trail in all its magnificence; 2) you'll avoid the crowds that concentrate at the bottom of The Narrows; 3) you can spend the night camping in The Narrows. While it's possible to hike The Narrows top-down in a single, exhausting day, I don't recommend it. You'll be rushing. Overnight camping lets you slow down, relax and spend two full days exploring and enjoying The Narrows. The only catch: permits, which are limited and hard to obtain in peak season. The park awards just 40 top-down Narrows permits each day (see following pages for details). But if you do snag that golden ticket, you'll be treated to uncrowded, scenic wonders that only a small fraction of Zion visitors ever experience.

TRAILHEAD The Narrows top-down starts at Chamberlain Ranch, located on the eastern edge of Zion National Park. Unless you have two cars, it's best to hire a private shuttle (p.14) to drop you off at the trailhead.

TRAIL INFO

RATING: Strenuous

DISTANCE: 16 miles

HIKING TIME: 1–2 days

ELEVATION CHANGE: 1,200 feet

Trail Description

TRAILHEAD, CHAMBERLAIN RANCH   The trailhead, located at Chamberlain Ranch, is a 1.5-hour drive from the Temple of Sinawava, where The Narrows ends. To get there drive 2.4 miles east of Zion's East Entrance Station, then turn left onto North Fork County Road. Drive 18 miles, cross a bridge, turn left, and drive one mile to the trailhead. The hike starts on dry ground, passing through a wide meadow before nearing the river.

BULLOCH'S CABIN (2 MILES) The trail drops towards the river near this old pioneer cabin. Although it's possible to hike alongside the river on dry ground, hiking in the river is fun and you'll have to do it eventually. Strap on your river shoes and start splashing. As you hike, keep your eyes out for a 50-foot natural rock arch above the right bank of the river.

FIRST NARROWS (6.1 MILES)   The rock walls on either side of the river have been rising higher and higher, but this is where the true Narrows begins. From here to the end, you're surrounded by towering cliffs.

WATERFALL (8.3 MILES) A gorgeous 12-foot waterfall (p.202) tumbles over a pile of rocks and logs at this narrow constriction in the canyon. Don't jump or scramble down the waterfall. There's an easy route to the left (south) through a cleft in the rocks.

DEEP CREEK CONFLUENCE (8.9 MILES) Deep Creek flows into the Virgin River at this wide junction, where the volume of water in The Narrows more than doubles. From this point on, swift currents and slippery rocks make hiking more challenging. Campsites are scattered along both sides of the river between Deep Creek and Big Spring.

BIG SPRING (11.5 MILES) This lush spring, which tumbles into the Virgin River in a series of beautiful waterfalls, marks the farthest point bottom-up day hikers can travel in The Narrows. Take a moment to enjoy the peace and quiet. You'll encounter progressively more day hikers the farther downstream you go.

ORDERVILLE CANYON (13.5 MILES)   This gorgeous side canyon is worth exploring if you've got the energy and there's still plenty of daylight.

MYSTERY FALLS (14.7 MILES) This thin ribbon of water tumbles down the side of a sloping cliff. Look for canyoneers rappelling down from Mystery Canyon.

RIVERSIDE WALKWAY (15.1 MILES) You know you're near the end of the trail when big crowds dressed in inadequate hiking gear stumble all around you. Eventually you'll round a corner and spot Riverside Walk (p.169), which heads to the Temple of Sinawava.

Permits

Permits are required for all Narrows top-down hikers, including both campers and one-day hikers. The park issues 40 permits per day; 24 are available three months in advance, 16 are reserved for last-minute lotteries. (See page 14 for more on permits.) Note: Even if you reserve a permit in advance, the park does not issue top-down permits when the Virgin River's flow is 120 cfs or higher.

Camping

There are 12 campsites for top-down hikers, all of which must be reserved when applying for a permit. Most campsites accommodate up to six people, but some can accommodate up to 12 people. (Visit jameskaiser.com for campsite photos and info.) Camping in The Narrows is limited to one night. In addition to normal camping gear, pack warm clothes, dry footwear, headlamps and a way to purify water. Fires are not allowed. All trash, food and human waste must be carried out. (Your best option is not pooping. Your second-best option is pooping in a sanitary bag, which the wilderness desk provides when it issues your permit. Extra sanitary bags are available at the Zion Visitor Center Store.)

Dangers

Top-down hikers face the same dangers as bottom-up hikers. See page 187.

Narrows Waterfall

❧ OBSERVATION POINT ❧

SUMMARY   Situated 2,000 feet above the northern end of Zion Canyon, Observation Point offers panoramic views of the park. As you gaze down the full length of Zion Canyon, dozens of peaks cascade towards the horizon. The most challenging and scenic route to Observation Point is a four-mile, one-way hike that starts at Weeping Rock (shuttle stop #7). As you ascend the trail, you'll pass through Echo Canyon (a dramatic, shadowy slot canyon), then climb a series of exposed switchbacks to the rim. At times, the dropoffs on the switchbacks are dramatic, but the trail is wide enough that even those with a fear of heights should feel comfortable. Once at the rim, it's an easy 0.8-mile stroll to the viewpoint, which sits on a rocky outcrop filled with juniper trees and piñon pines. A second, significantly easier route to Observation Point starts at the East Mesa trailhead (p.206).

WEEPING ROCK TRAILHEAD   The Observation Point Trail starts at Weeping Rock Shuttle Stop #7. From the parking area, cross the small footbridge and bear right.

TRAIL INFO

RATING: Strenuous   **DISTANCE:** 8 miles, round-trip

HIKING TIME: 4–5 hours   **ELEVATION CHANGE:** 2,150 feet

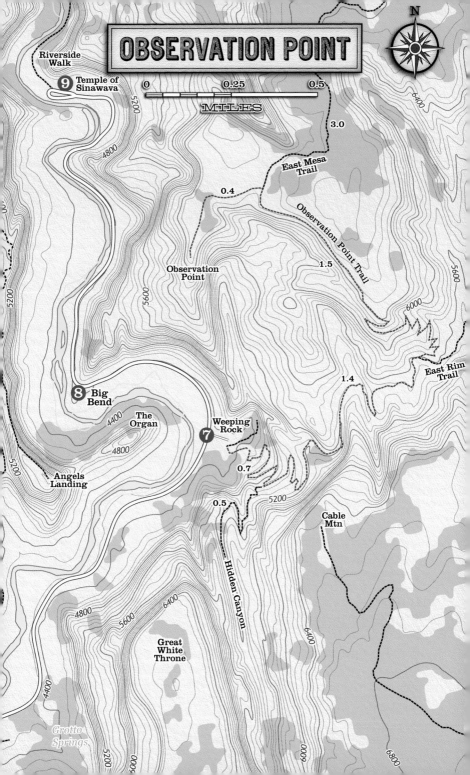

OBSERVATION POINT

N

Riverside
Walk

9 Temple of
Sinawava

MILES

0   0.25   0.5

3.0

East Mesa
Trail

0.4

Observation Point Trail

Observation
Point

1.5

6400

5200

4800

5600

5200

5200

6000

5600

East Rim
Trail

1.4

8 Big
Bend

The
Organ

7 Weeping
Rock

4400

4800

0.7

Angels
Landing

5200

0.5

5200

Cable
Mtn

Hidden Canyon

4800

5600

6400

Great
White
Throne

4400

6400

Grotto
Springs

5200

5600

6000

6000

6800

Hiking through Echo Canyon

Alternate Route to Observation Point: East Mesa Trail

SUMMARY If the splendid views from Observation Point sound intriguing— but hiking four miles and 2,000 vertical feet does not—there is an alternative. The East Mesa Trail, which starts at the park's eastern boundary, lies 3.3 miles from Observation Point and its elevation change is just 250 feet. While others are huffing and puffing up switchbacks, you'll be whistling while you walk. Of course, the East Mesa Trail isn't nearly as scenic as the Observation Point Trail. But what it lacks in scenery, it more than makes up for in ease to your knees. Drive to the trailhead (one hour from Springdale) for an out-and-back hike, or hire a shuttle (p.14) to drop you off at the trailhead, then hike down Observation Point Trail to Weeping Rock, where you can catch the free park shuttle.

TRAILHEAD Drive 2.4 miles east of Zion's East Entrance, then turn left onto North Fork County Road. Drive 5.4 miles to Ponderosa Ranch, then follow the signs to East Mesa Trailhead. High clearance is required for the final, bumpy stretch, which is sometimes compromised by mud, snow or ice.

TRAIL INFO

RATING: Easy   **DISTANCE:** 6.6 miles round-trip

HIKING TIME: 3 hours   **ELEVATION CHANGE:** 250 feet

Switchbacks blasted into the rock on the Observation Point Trail

⊰ HIDDEN CANYON ⊱

SUMMARY This lovely, uncrowded slot canyon is located halfway up the steep cliffs above Weeping Rock. Although strolling along the flat, sandy floor of the canyon is easy, getting there requires hiking over 800 vertical feet, then traversing a short ledge with steep, scary dropoffs. Chains bolted into the rock serve as handholds. Although similar to the chains on Angels Landing, the chains on Hidden Canyon's exposed ledge are significantly shorter and less intimidating. It's a great test run if you're unsure about hiking Angels Landing. Once past the ledge, the trail tucks into Hidden Canyon, which cuts between Cable Mountain and the Great White Throne. In places you'll need to scramble over small rocks and logs. About 0.3 miles down Hidden Canyon there's a ground-level rock arch on the right. A short distance later a metal sign marks the point where further travel is prohibited. The remainder of Hidden Canyon is off limits to protect Mexican spotted owls (p.83).

TRAILHEAD The trail starts at Weeping Rock (shuttle stop #7). Follow the Observation Point Trail 0.7 miles, then turn right onto the Hidden Canyon Trail.

◆ TRAIL INFO ◆

RATING: Strenuous

DISTANCE: 2 miles round-trip

HIKING TIME: 3 hours

ELEVATION CHANGE: 850 feet

∼❧ WEST RIM (BOTTOM-UP) ❧∼

SUMMARY   The West Rim Trail (p.260) twists and turns through some of the park's most magnificent scenery, but most people ignore the bottom-up route even though it starts in Zion Canyon. Why? Because to get to the West Rim Trail from Zion Canyon you must first pass Angels Landing, whose gravitational pull sucks in 99% of selfie-snapping hikers. But if you have the social media fortitude to pass Angels Landing at Scout Lookout—zigging where others zag—you'll discover a stunning, crowd-free canyon surrounded by towering cliffs and blanketed with rolling sandstone. Hike at least one mile past Scout Lookout for beautiful views of this "hidden" landscape. For a strenuous hike, continue another two miles and 1,000 vertical feet to Cabin Spring, located near a spectacular view-point (see following page). From this vantage point you'll enjoy sweeping views of the canyon below.

TRAILHEAD   The trail to West Rim Trail starts at The Grotto (shuttle stop #6). It follows the same route as Angels Landing, then veers left at Scout Lookout.

TRAIL INFO

RATING: Strenuous   **DISTANCE:** 6–10 miles round-trip

HIKING TIME: 5–8 hours   **ELEVATION CHANGE:** 2,500 feet

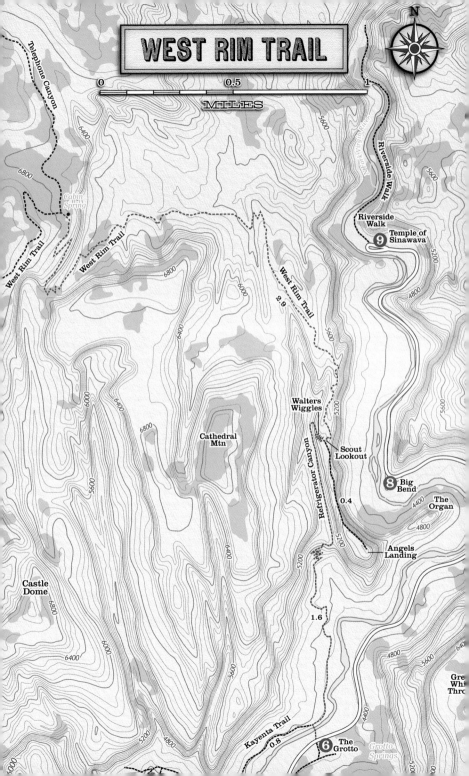

View near Cabin Spring

EAST ZION

IF ZION CANYON didn't exist, East Zion would still be worthy of national park status. The same rocks that form sheer cliffs in Zion Canyon blanket East Zion in vast, rolling waves of sandstone. A 10-mile road weaves through the Martian landscape, providing access to great hikes, fabulous slot canyons, and stunning slickrock scenery.

East Zion was largely inaccessible until the Zion Tunnel connected it to Zion Canyon in 1930. Blasted through a mile of solid rock, the tunnel is an engineering marvel. To get there from Canyon Junction, follow the Zion-Mount Carmel Highway (State Route 9) up 3.6 miles of hairpin turns with fabulous, vertigo-inducing views. Entering the tunnel feels like entering a wormhole—which, in a sense, you are because you're driving through the petrified remains of 200-million year-old sand dunes!

After a few dark minutes you'll emerge into a brilliant, geologic wonderland. The road twists above narrow Clear Creek drainage, with deep side canyons branching off in all directions. There's a good chance you'll see people wearing wetsuits, helmets and harnesses on the side of the road. They are canyoneers exploring East Zion's fabulous (and chilly and wet) slot canyons (p.23).

The farther you drive, the more open and dramatic the scenery becomes. Feel free to park at any of the unmarked pullouts on the side of the road and explore the landscape. Although there's lots of great hiking in East Zion, there are few official trails. Canyon Overlook (p.223) is the most famous hike, but I've also included some interesting, lesser-known hikes on the following pages.

Located roughly 1,000 feet above Zion Canyon, East Zion has a higher-elevation ecology speckled with piñon pines and juniper trees. In October scattered hardwoods shimmer with brilliant foliage. No matter when you visit keep your eyes out for bighorn sheep (p.88), which were reintroduced in 1972 after severe population declines. Today East Zion is the best place in the park to see these majestic animals.

In many ways, East Zion is a world apart from Zion Canyon. There are no shuttles, restaurants or gift shops. There's not even drinking water. But that's what makes it special. Whether you enjoy the rugged scenery from the road or venture into the wilderness, East Zion is not to be missed.

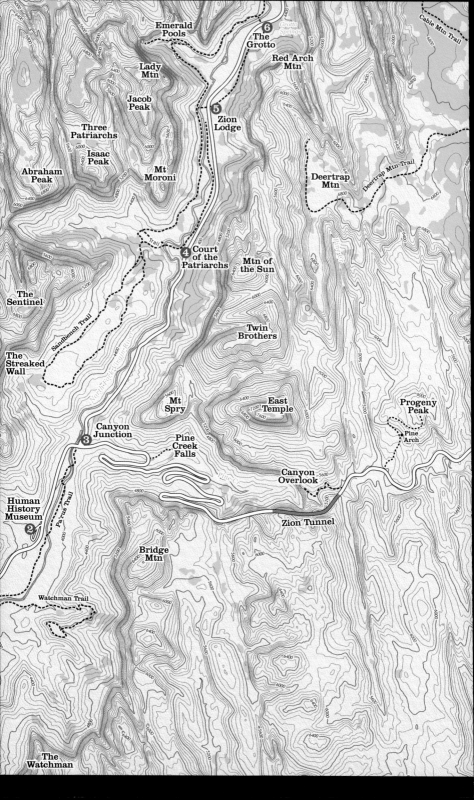

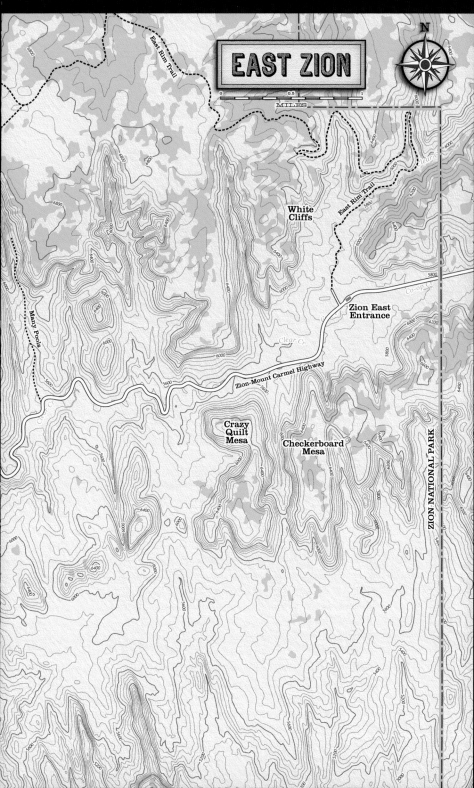

Pine Creek Falls

Great Arch

Pine Creek Falls

This "hidden" waterfall is a worthy destination that's unmarked and easy to miss, which helps keeps down the crowds. From Canyon Junction drive half a mile east to the first major bend in the road. The 0.3-mile trail starts next to a small parking area. After heading east through the vegetation, you'll follow the banks of Pine Creek, which are relatively easy to hike at low water levels but require more rock scrambling at higher flows. There are unofficial routes on both sides of the creek, but conditions vary. Use your judgement. Eventually you'll arrive at a beautiful alcove with a two-tier waterfall tumbling into a shallow pool.

Great Arch

At 600 feet wide by 400 feet high, Great Arch is one of the most impressive formations in Zion. Towering above the eastern end of Pine Creek Canyon, this massive rock arch looks more dramatic the higher you drive. This is an excellent example of a "blind arch" (or "inset arch") where just one side is exposed—as opposed to a freestanding arch that's open on both sides. Great Arch is located just above the boundary of Navajo Sandstone and Kayenta Formation. As the softer Kayenta Formation eroded under the harder Navajo Sandstone, the unsupported sandstone collapsed along cracks in the rock. Arches are naturally strong, so erosion often favors arch formation. You can test the strength yourself by hiking the Canyon Overlook Trail (p.223), which ends on top of Great Arch.

Zion Tunnel

Stretching 1.1 miles through solid rock, the Zion Tunnel provides a shortcut to East Zion through the park's otherwise impenetrable cliffs. The history of its construction is as fascinating as the tunnel itself.

When Zion became a national park in 1919, park officials wanted to make Zion Canyon more accessible from the east. But the rugged geology blocked any logical route. A local cattle rancher, John Winder, had a novel idea: Why not build a road up Pine Creek Canyon to Great Arch, then blast a tunnel through the center of the arch? Two government engineers, Howard Means and B.J. Finch, studied Winder's idea and agreed with the basic concept, but they concluded the tunnel should be built through cliffs adjacent to the arch.

Work began in 1927. An aerial tram with a 1,200-foot cable transported workers and supplies to a temporary camp 400 feet above the canyon floor. More than 100 men were split into two crews. One crew worked on the switchbacks rising 800 feet from the Virgin River to the Navajo Sandstone cliffs. The other crew blasted the tunnel into the sandstone—a job requiring nearly 300,000 pounds of dynamite. Workers first blasted large openings, or "galleries," into the side of the cliffs, then connected the galleries from the inside. This technique, called "ring drilling," was pioneered by the mining industry, but it had never been used to build a highway tunnel. Working day and night, the tunnel crew burrowed 5,613 feet in 313 days.

Next, construction crews drove through the tunnel to begin work on a road through East Zion. The job required blasting through slickrock, construction of multiple bridges, and drilling a second, shorter tunnel. When finished, the highway stretched 25 miles from Zion Canyon to Route 89 in Mount Carmel.

On July 4, 1930, the Zion-Mount Carmel Highway and Tunnel officially opened. Over 2,000 people attended the dedication ceremony, including governors from 20 states. The total cost was nearly $2 million (about $25 million today). The Zion Tunnel was the longest tunnel in the United States, and the new highway shortened the driving distance from Zion to Bryce Canyon by more than 60 miles. The following year, visitation to Bryce Canyon jumped 60%.

When the Zion Tunnel first opened, traffic was minimal and visitors could park at the viewing galleries to enjoy the dramatic views. As traffic increased—and vehicles grew larger—the tunnel struggled to cope. Today cars must drive through the tunnel without stopping, and oversized vehicles like RVs are required to use the One-Way Traffic Control Service provided by the Park (p.31).

The Zion Tunnel is the longest tunnel in any national park and the eighth-longest highway tunnel in America. Newer, modern tunnels may be longer and larger, but the Zion Tunnel was remarkable for its time. In 2011 the American Society of Civil Engineers declared it a historic landmark.

West
Temple

Sundial

Altar of
Sacrifice

Beehives

Streaked
Wall

Canyon Overlook

Perched on top of Great Arch (p.219), Canyon Overlook is the most popular hike in East Zion and one of the most dramatic viewpoints in the park. The trail, which starts near Zion Tunnel's east entrance, is a moderately easy one-mile stroll out and back. Often the most challenging part is finding parking. There's a small parking area directly across from the trailhead (which can be entered only after exiting the Zion Tunnel) and another parking area 600 feet northeast.

From the trailhead, stone steps lead to a series of semi-exposed ledges. Metal railings provide protection at particularly steep sections. Soon you'll round a corner, cross a small bridge, and wrap around a shadowy, recessed alcove. The trail continues, with occasional mild scrambling, until you reach the top of Great Arch. Whimsical rock formations surround the viewpoint. Spread out below is Pine Creek Canyon. In the distance, forming a 3,000-foot wall against the western horizon, are the Towers of the Virgin (p.138). Views are terrific throughout the day, but Canyon Overlook is particularly popular at sunset. If you visit for sunset try to arrive early to beat the crowds.

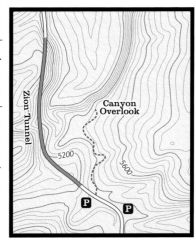

Pine Arch & Progeny Peak

This unnamed peak (dubbed Progeny Peak by local hikers) rises over 1,000 feet above the road and offers stunning, 360-degree views of East Zion. About halfway up there's a freestanding rock arch (originally called Two Pines Arch, but one of the pines has fallen). There is no official trail up the slickrock. The half-mile hike to Pine Arch is relatively easy with some moderate scrambling near the end. The three-quarter-mile hike to Progeny Peak is a strenuous scramble with steep dropoffs. It should only be attempted by those with previous route-finding experience in Zion or similar desert environments.

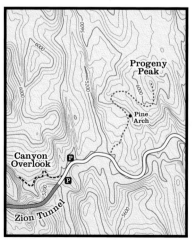

The route starts 0.4 miles north of the Canyon Overlook parking area on the north side of the road. Drop into the wash, hike north, and bear right when the wash splits in two. Keep your eyes out for the rock arch, which becomes easier to spot as you approach the cliffs where it's located. From the arch head north to a series of rock ledges that rise towards Progeny Peak. Be sure to spend plenty of time finding the safest route, and don't hesitate to backtrack. The final push to the summit is best attempted just south of the peak.

Pine Arch

Many Pools

One of the most interesting hikes in East Zion is the slickrock canyon known as Many Pools. Cascading through the heart of the canyon are dozens of small pools, linked by ephemeral ribbons of water, that fill during spring runoff or after heavy rains. During extended dry spells, some pools run low or disappear entirely. The two-mile route to the top of Many Pools is a moderate hike with occasional scrambling. The unmarked trailhead is located 0.8 miles east of East Zion's second short tunnel, across from a parking area on the south side of the

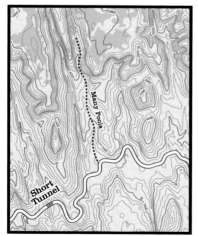

road. Drop into the wash, hike up the center of the canyon, and after a few minutes you'll encounter the first pools. The farther you hike, the prettier the pools become. The route ends after roughly one mile near a dozen closely-spaced pools.

As you hike alongside the pools, gaze into the water. Sometimes you can see frogs, tadpoles or tiny crustaceans. In the desert, even tiny pockets of water can sustain unlikely animals. Some crustaceans survive extended droughts by dehydrating completely. They can lie dormant for decades, then spring to life as soon as water becomes available.

"Rolling masses of cumuli rose up into the blue to incomprehensible heights ... As they drifted rapidly against the great barrier, the currents from below flung upward to the summits, rolled the vaporous massses into vast whorls, wrapping them around the towers and crest-lines, and scattering torn shreds of mist along the rock faces ... they rallied their black forces for a more desperate struggle, and answered with defiant flashes of lightning the incessant pour of sun-shafts."

—Clarence Dutton, 1880

Checkerboard Mesa

East Zion is filled with striking geology, but Checkerboard Mesa is in a class of its own. Rising to an elevation of 6,670 feet (2,033 meters), the mesa's bold geometry commands your attention as you drive along the road. From its narrow, forested top, an enormous sandstone skirt slopes down at a nearly uniform angle and wraps around a massive, oval base. Vertical cracks intersect with horizontal lines to form a monumental, convex "checkerboard." This distinctive pattern is the result of two types of erosion: horizontal cross-bedding formed by ancient sand dunes (p.52) and vertical cracking due to expansion and contraction. As sunlight heats the rock, it expands and cracks. Cold temperatures, by contrast, compress the rock. This ongoing compression/expansion cycle slowly increases the size of the cracks. Rain and melting snow also flow into the cracks and increase erosion through the freeze/thaw cycle.

Most visitors view Checkerboard Mesa from the parking area 1,000 feet north of its base. But it's worth exploring the rock patterns up close to fully appreciate their magnitude. There's a pullout near the base from which you can scramble up the slickrock. With two dozen friends dressed in black and red you could conceivably play human checkers. Lying just west of Checkerboard Mesa is a similar cross-hatched formation dubbed Crazy Quilt Mesa. Between them lies Checkerboard Mesa Canyon. Although there's no official trail through Checkerboard Mesa Canyon, some faint unofficial trails meander across the slickrock canyon.

⊰ CABLE MOUNTAIN ⊱

SUMMARY Towering above Weeping Rock, Cable Mountain offers stunning views from its sheer ledge, which plunges nearly 2,000 feet to Zion Canyon's floor. There are many ledges with steep dropoffs in Zion, but Cable Mountain is one of the steepest. That's why local entrepreneur David Flanigan built a cableworks in 1901 to transport lumber from the rim (where ponderosa pines are abundant) to the valley floor (where trees for lumber are scarce). decaying remains are still perched on the edge of the cliff. The real highlight, however, is the dramatic view of Zion Canyon—particularly Angels Landing and the rocky spine that leads to its summit. Although you can hike to Cable Mountain from Weeping Rock (7.7 miles, 1,950 vertical feet), a much easier route starts from the Stave Spring Trailhead on Zion's eastern boundary (one-hour drive from Springdale).

TRAILHEAD Drive 2.4 miles east of Zion's East Entrance, then turn left onto North Fork County Road. Drive 5.4 miles to Ponderosa Ranch. Follow the signs to Cable Mountain. High clearance required just before the trailhead.

TRAIL INFO

RATING: Moderate

DISTANCE: 7.2 miles round-trip

HIKING TIME: 4–5 hours

ELEVATION CHANGE: 500 feet

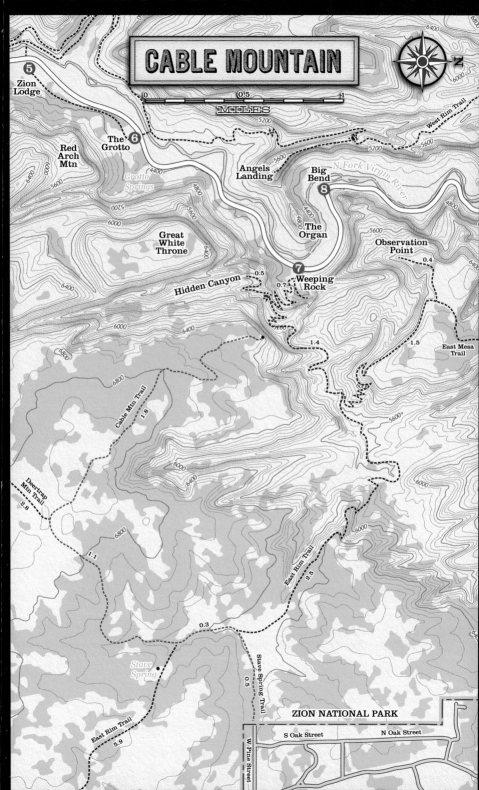

View from Cable Mountain

❧ DEERTRAP MOUNTAIN ❧

SUMMARY There are plenty of great hikes at the northern end of Zion Canyon, but Deertrap Mountain, which rises above Zion Lodge, offers rare views of the canyon's central and southwest sections. The trail to Deertrap Mountain (named because Southern Paiute hunters once herded deer into a trap on the mountain) starts at Stave Spring Trailhead. It follows the same route to Cable Mountain, then veers left at a signed junction 1.8 miles from the trailhead. After passing through a dense patch of Gambel oak, you'll skirt the rim of East Zion before descending toward the rim of Zion Canyon. The first overlook on Deertrap Mountain offers expansive views stretching west to Zion Canyon's entrance. The best views, however, are yet to come. Follow the path north roughly half a mile to a rocky promontory with panoramic views of central Zion Canyon, including head-on views of Angels Landing.

TRAILHEAD Drive 2.4 miles east of Zion's East Entrance, then turn left onto North Fork County Road. Drive 5.4 miles to Ponderosa Ranch. Follow the signs to Cable Mountain. High clearance is required to reach Stave Spring Trailhead.

TRAIL INFO

RATING: Moderate

DISTANCE: 9 miles round-trip

HIKING TIME: 5–6 hours

ELEVATION CHANGE: 420 feet

❧ EAST RIM TRAIL ☙

SUMMARY The East Rim Trail isn't as famous as the West Rim Trail, but it offers similar scenery with fewer crowds. Although you can hike the East Rim Trail in a single, exhausting day, it's best done as a two-day backpack (permits required). By splitting the hike into two days, you'll have plenty of time to make side trips to Cable Mountain or Deertrap Mountain. From the East Rim trailhead the trail rises 1,000 feet above East Zion's dramatic slickrock into the forested mesa that divides East Zion from Zion Canyon. Nestled among tall ponderosa pines is Stave Spring, which offers a reliable water source for backpackers. The East Rim Trail then descends into Echo Canyon, a stunning expanse of rolling sandstone that, although physically close to Zion Canyon, is overlooked by most visitors. The trail eventually connects with the Observation Point Trail, which ends at Weeping Rock (shuttle stop #7).

TRAILHEAD Roughly 150 yards west of the East Zion Entrance Station, a spur road heads to the parking area where the East Rim Trail begins.

◀ TRAIL INFO ▶

RATING: Strenuous

HIKING TIME: 1–2 Days

DISTANCE: 10.8 miles

ELEVATION CHANGE: 2,300 feet

East Rim Trail Description

TRAILHEAD Roughly 150 yards west of the Zion East Entrance, a short road heads north to the East Rim Trailhead. From the parking area follow the sandy trail, which was originally an old Southern Paiute route. The trail twists and turns above Clear Creek, then starts its long ascent to the forests above. In spring, blooming cliffrose perfumes the trail.

JOLLEY GULCH (2.6 MILES) As the trail rounds a tight corner, you'll pass the steep dropoff to Jolley Gulch. Watch your step! There is no protective barrier and its a *long* way down. In the distance you can see Checkerboard Mesa and the dramatic cliffs of East Zion. A nearly perfect line separates the top layer of Navajo Sandstone from the Temple Cap Formation above, marking the point, 160 million years ago, when the Sundance Sea washed over Utah.

STAVE SPRING (5.3 MILES) Nestled among a grove of tall ponderosa pines, Stave Spring is the only reliable water source on the trail. The spring—little more than a trickle of water in dry years—flows from a pipe into a puddle. Be sure to treat or filter the water before drinking. Backpackers must camp at least 1/4 mile from the spring.

CABLE MOUNTAIN JUNCTION (5.4 MILES) At this junction a trail veers left (south) to Cable Mountain and Deertrap Mountain, both of which make excellent side trips if you're backpacking.

STAVE SPRING TRAILHEAD JUNCTION (5.8 MILES) After huffing and puffing 1,000 vertical feet, you may be surprised to see energetic day hikers casually strolling along the trail. They likely arrived from Stave Spring Trailhead, a vehicle-accessible trailhead located just 0.3 miles east of this junction.

ECHO CANYON RIM (6.2 MILES) From here the trail plunges nearly 2,000 feet to the floor of Echo Canyon. Along the way you'll enjoy dramatic views of sheer cliffs and rolling sandstone. Near the floor of the canyon the trail sometimes becomes faint. Look for cairns (small rock piles) that guide hikers along the official trail.

OBSERVATION POINT TRAIL JUNCTION (7.8 MILES) After rounding a corner the East Rim Trail ends at a junction with Observation Point Trail. Brace yourself. The sudden surge of Observation Point day hikers can be a shock to your wilderness-mellowed synapses.

ECHO CANYON (8.8 MILES) This dramatic slot canyon offers a bit of shade and some fascinating geology.

WEEPING ROCK (10.8 MILES) Your wilderness adventure officially ends at the Weeping Rock shuttle stop.

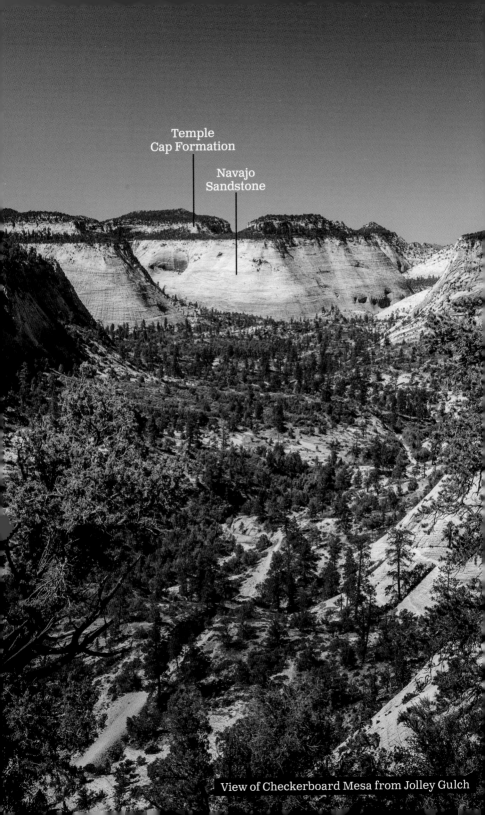

Temple
Cap Formation

Navajo
Sandstone

View of Checkerboard Mesa from Jolley Gulch

SOUTHWEST DESERT

Situated in the arid lowlands along the park's southern boundary, the Southwest Desert is Zion's most overlooked and underappreciated region. Which is exactly why some people love it. You can still enjoy Zion's soaring sandstone cliffs, which rise above the northern horizon, combined with gorgeous views of the Virgin River Valley, which yawns open to reveal a classic Western mosaic of crumbly mesas and buttes. The ample spaces and unique ecology attract a different kind of visitor—more interested in serenity than selfies.

The highlight of Zion's Southwest Desert is the Chinle Trail (p.246), which wraps around the base of Mount Kinesava en route to Coalpits Wash. Petrified logs, the remnants of 220-million-year-old trees buried in the Chinle Rock Formation, are scattered along the trail, and there are a half-dozen campsites for backpackers. Just west of the Chinle Trail is Crater Hill (p.243), an ancient volcano that erupted 100,000 years ago.

Zion's Southwest Desert brushes against the northeastern tip of the Mojave Desert, North America's smallest, driest desert. Covering 50,000 miles in California, Nevada, Arizona and a sliver of southwest Utah, the Mojave is famous for Joshua trees, whose range roughly marks the boundary of the desert. There are no Joshua trees in Zion—the closest are in Saint George—but there are plenty of other beautiful desert plants. Prince's plume (p.75) and milkvetch grow in the selenium-rich soils of eroded Chinle rocks. (Milkvetch is also known as "locoweed" due to the effects of selenium in the plant.) Dozens of desert wildflowers bloom here in spring, with peak blooms normally occurring in April.

Some fascinating animals also call the Southwest Desert home. The threatened Mojave desert tortoise (p.100) reaches the northeast limit of its range in Zion. Under ideal conditions desert tortoises can live nearly a century, but juvenile tortoises must avoid predators such as Gila monsters (p.98), the largest lizard native to the United States. Growing up to two feet long, Gila monsters also reach the northeast limit of their range in Zion. Both reptiles are rarely seen, but that's part of what makes this region special. The seemingly barren landscape is filled with hidden surprises.

Crater Hill

Today most visitors rush along Route 9 between Virgin and Rockville, giving little thought to the surrounding landscape. But 100,000 years ago this was the scene of one of Zion's most splendid catastrophes. As tectonic plates shifted, lava poured out of cracks in the earth, forming a large cinder cone called Crater Hill (left). As lava flowed south from Crater Hill into the Virgin River, it boiled the water and formed a 400-foot dam near the present-day ghost town of Grafton. The dam backed up an ancient lake that may have covered ten square miles and stretched all the way to the Zion Canyon Visitor Center. But over thousands of years the Virgin River eroded the dam and drained the lake.

⊰ CHINLE TRAIL ⊱

SUMMARY   Wrapping around the base of Mount Kinesava, whose sandstone cliffs rise 7,285 feet above sea level, the Chinle Trail is the Southwest Desert's most popular hike. Due to its relatively low elevation, summer temperatures are extremely hot, but the trail's warmer temperatures are a blessing in the cooler months. From the trailhead just below a high-end subdivision, the Chinle Trail twists along a wash and crosses a bridge before heading towards the Zion wilderness. En route to Coalpits Wash you'll pass a mix of cacti, shrubs and piñon/juniper forest. Huber Wash, a deep gully that adds a bit of visual drama to the flatlands, makes a great destination for day hikers (3.3 miles one way, 3–4 hours). Just beyond Huber Wash, fragments of petrified wood can be found along the side of the trail. Backpackers can camp at one of a half-dozen campsites. Note: The Chinle Trail can get very muddy after a heavy rain.

TRAILHEAD   The Chinle Trails starts from a dirt parking area just below the Anasazi Way Subdivision. The turnoff is located four miles southwest of Zion's South Entrance off State Route 9.

TRAIL INFO

RATING: Moderate

HIKING TIME: 2–8 hours

DISTANCE: 8.1 miles one way

ELEVATION CHANGE: 200 feet

KOLOB TERRACE

THESE GORGEOUS HIGHLANDS, located west of Zion Canyon, shelter some of Zion's most beautiful, overlooked scenery. Kolob Terrace Road rises more than 4,000 feet from the Mojave Desert to an alpine forest of ponderosa pines and quaking aspen. Driving the 21-mile road is the ecological equivalent of traveling from Utah to Canada in less than an hour.

Your adventure starts in the 600-person town of Virgin (which famously passed a law in 2000 requiring every adult resident to possess a firearm). To get to Virgin from Springdale, drive 13 miles west along Route 9. Turn right onto Kolob Terrace Road and ascend the dramatic canyon carved by North Creek. The road levels out in Cave Valley, a peaceful flatland surrounding by surreal rock formations, then continues its ascent. As you rise into alpine forest, the scenery becomes more like the Rockies than the desert Southwest.

Zion National Park acquired this land in the 1950s, and it remains a bit of a patchwork. As you drive along Kolob Terrace Road, you'll pass in and out of the park. Some of the non-park land is privately owned (hence the luxury homes and wandering cattle) and some belongs to the Bureau of Land Management (which, unlike Zion, allows guides to take clients canyoneering and rock climbing). The Zion sections offer access to some of the park's most famous hikes, including strenuous treks like The Subway (p.256) and the West Rim Trail (p.260). For a beautiful, easy stroll consider Northgate Peaks (p.266).

Most visitors drive as far as Lava Point (p.255), a sweeping 7,890-foot viewpoint near a small first-come, first-served campground. The last four miles of Kolob Terrace Road head to Kolob Reservoir, a manmade lake popular with anglers. No matter how far you go, try to head back in the late afternoon. With plenty of clear western views, the light on Kolob Terrace Road is stunning in the late afternoon and at sunset.

In summer, when Zion Canyon is hot and crowded, Kolob Terrace enjoys cooler temperatures and limited crowds. In autumn you'll enjoy beautiful foliage that peaks about a week or two before the foliage in Zion Canyon. Winter is also beautiful, but from late November to early May, Lava Point is often inaccessible because of deep winter snow.

Kolob Terrace Road

From the town of Virgin, Kolob Terrace Road rises above North Creek between the cliffs of Cougar Mountain to the east and Smith Mesa to the west. At times the road travels along a narrow strip of black rock just a few yards across with steep dropoffs on either side. This unusual topography is a textbook example of what geologists call an "inverted valley." Between 300,000 and 200,000 years ago, volcanoes erupted at Firepit Knoll and Spendlove Knoll, spewing lava into an ancient river valley. When the lava cooled, the river valley was filled with a hard dark rock called basalt. Over the past 200,000 years, as soft sedimentary rock eroded around the hard basalt, twin drainages formed on either side. Eventually the ancient basalt eroded to a narrow strip above the new drainages, and today lower Kolob Terrace Road travels along this ancient lava flow.

Drive higher and you'll pass through a unusual landscape filled with charred trees. These are the remains of the 2006 Kolob Fire, which burned over 17,000 acres—the largest wildfire in park history. Most Zion wildfires occur above 6,500 feet in ponderosa pine forest. The Kolob Fire was the first Zion wildfire in lower elevation piñon-juniper forest since European settlement. Although sparked by humans, its extreme devastation was fueled by cheatgrass, a highly flammable invasive species that has displaced native grasses in much of the park. Following the Kolob Fire, the park spread native seeds over hundreds of acres to help restore native plants.

Altar of Sacrifice   West Temple   Mount Kinesava   Tabernacle Dome

Cave Valley

After a 10-mile drive from the town of Virgin, Kolob Terrace Road flattens out in Cave Valley. Located at an elevation of 6,000 feet and surrounded by Seussian rock formations, this long grassy valley is particularly dramatic in early morning or late afternoon when golden light illuminates the Navajo Sandstone. As you enter Cave Valley, the rounded profile of Tabernacle Dome appears on your right. Named for its resemblance to the Mormon Tabernacle Dome in Salt Lake City, this imposing rock formation marks the southeastern end of the valley. Looming beyond Tabernacle Dome to the southeast are the sheer white cliffs of the Towers of the Virgin (p.138), offering backside views of Mount Kinesava, West Temple and the Altar of Sacrifice.

A rock formation called Lambs Knoll rises above the western edge of Cave Valley. Filled with accessible steep walls and narrow slot canyons, Lambs Knoll is a popular spot for beginning rock climbers and canyoneers. Because it's located just outside the boundaries of Zion National Park, local outfitters can offer guided rock climbing and canyoneering lessons here. A dirt road leads to a large parking area near the base of Lambs Knoll.

Cave Valley is part of the checkerboard pattern of private land adjacent to Zion National Park. As you drive along Kolob Terrace Road you'll pass vacation homes and grazing cattle. Cave Valley is named after caves in the surrounding rock formations.

Firepit Knoll

Hoodoos

One of the most striking features of Kolob Terrace Road is the abundance of hoodoos: stubby, whimsical rock formations scattered throughout the landscape. Also called fairy chimneys, hoodoos form when soft rock is capped by harder, more erosion-resistant rock. As the landscape erodes, the hard rock erodes at a slower rate, protecting patches of underlying soft rock which form rocky pinnacles (hoodoos). The world's most famous hoodoos are found at Bryce Canyon National Park, but there are plenty scattered around Zion as well. This is particularly true at high elevations, where melting snow and the freeze/thaw cycle tend to accelerate erosion.

One of the best places to examine hoodoos up-close is the sandstone knoll just north of Hop Valley Trailhead. Drive a quarter-mile past the trailhead and look for a small pullout on the left side of Kolob Terrace Road. From the pullout, scramble down to a gorgeous patch of slickrock, whose magnificent cross-bedding reveals the contours of ancient sand dunes (p.52). Continue northwest towards the gentle, stairstep bowl that leads to the top of the knoll, where you can examine the fabulous hoodoos up close. You'll also enjoy terrific, elevated views of the landscape. The rounded hill to the northeast, called Firepit Knoll, is an ancient volcano that erupted 300,000 years ago. Across the road to the south is Spendlove Knoll, another ancient volcano that erupted 220,000 years ago. To the northwest you can make out the Hop Valley Trail (p.268) as it heads towards Kolob Canyons (p.273).

West
Temple

View from Lava Point

The
Narrows

Temple of
Sinawava

Lava Point

At 7,890 feet above sea level, Lava Point is the highest viewpoint in Zion National Park, with expansive views stretching nearly from Bryce Canyon to Grand Canyon. Set back from the viewpoint are a handful of picnic tables nestled under tall ponderosa pines. A short path heads to Lava Point Campground, which has six first-come, first-served campsites and pit toilets.

Lava Point is named for a lava flow that covered the land roughly one million years ago. The lava erupted from an ancient volcano at Home Valley Knoll, one mile west of Lava Point, and flowed 13 miles down the Left Fork of North Creek (p.256) to the present-day town of Virgin. When the lava cooled it created a hard protective layer over soft sedimentary rocks. Over the past million years, as the surrounding landscape eroded, Lava Point resisted erosion, leaving it perched high above the landscape.

Looking out from Lava Point, it's easy to understand why geologists call this region the Grand Staircase (p.55). To the east are the Pink Cliffs that characterize Bryce Canyon. Further down to the south lie the dramatic White Cliffs of Zion, including West Temple, the highest point in Zion Canyon. (At 7,810 feet, West Temple is just 80 feet shorter than Lava Point.) Beyond the White Cliffs lies the Kaibab Plateau, which forms the North Rim of Grand Canyon. Although there's plenty to see on the ground, don't forget to look up. The skies above are popular with endangered California condors (p.84). Zion rangers once counted 42 condors at Lava Point!

☙ THE SUBWAY (BOTTOM-UP) ❧

SUMMARY The Subway is one of Zion's geologic marvels—a curved, hollowed-out canyon, reminiscent of a subway tunnel, that's among the park's most photographed destinations. A series of cascading pools, exquisitely sculpted into the bedrock, add to its mystical allure. To get there, you'll need to descend a steep canyon, then hike three to five hours alongside the Left Fork of North Creek. The rugged trail, which is faint in places, has multiple river crossings. I highly recommend closed-toe water shoes and hiking poles. Despite the challenge of getting there, The Subway is so popular that permits are required for day hikers (p.14). The park service allocates 60 Subway permits a day, most of which are granted through a lottery three months in advance. A lottery for the remaining permits is open seven to two days in advance. Note: The Subway top-down route (which also requires a permit) involves technical canyoneering (p.23).

TRAILHEAD The Subway Trailhead (technically the Left Fork Trailhead) starts from a small parking area off Kolob Reservoir Road. The turnoff is 8.3 miles north of the intersection with Route 9 in the small town of Virgin.

TRAIL INFO

RATING: Strenuous   **DISTANCE:** 9 miles round-trip

HIKING TIME: 6–10 hours   **ELEVATION CHANGE:** 1,000 feet

Subway (Bottom-Up) Description

TRAILHEAD The Left Fork (Subway) trailhead is located off Kolob Reservoir Road, 8.3 miles north of the junction with Route 9 in the town of Virgin. From the parking area the trail drops through a piñon-juniper forest as it approaches the rim of Great West Canyon. The route is fairly obvious, but a sandy wash littered with footprints sometimes lures hikers off trail.

CANYON RIM (0.5 MILES) From the canyon rim it's a steep hike down to the Left Fork of North Creek. Compacted red dirt is interspaced with log steps, but in places the trail is steep, loose and crumbly. Use great caution at sections near dropoffs. Hiking poles are helpful.

JUNCTION WITH RIVER (1 MILE) This junction is hard to miss on the way down but easy to miss on the way back. Scan your surroundings and take a strong mental note. Even better, take a photo with your phone. From this point the trail parallels the river bank with some occasional stream crossings. Follow the well-traveled path, which is often marked with cairns (small stone piles). If you get confused, don't hesitate to backtrack to reorient yourself. Another option is strapping on water shoes and splashing upstream through the river.

DINOSAUR TRACKS (1.7 MILES) On the left (north) side of the river, two slabs of light-colored Kayenta Formation rock contain dinosaur footprints. The tracks probably belonged to a theropod, a three-toed dinosaur suborder that included velociraptors and Tyrannosaurus rex.

RED WATERFALLS (4.3 MILES) A series of beautiful waterfalls cascades over delicate layers of red rock. Most hikers, determined to reach the Subway, march right past them, which is a shame because they're a worthy destination on their own. Take some time to enjoy the tranquil scenery.

THE SUBWAY (4.5 MILES) After rounding a sharp bend, the curved, streaked walls of The Subway appear. As you continue upstream, undulating walls envelop the canyon, nearly blocking out the sun. You are now *inside* the Subway. A cascading series of "potholes" shelter cold, clear pools a few feet deep. Watch your step—the floor of The Subway is often wet and slippery. Deep pools eventually block further progress on foot, but swimmers can continue to a nice waterfall. Pass through the curtain of water to explore a hidden alcove known as the Waterfall Room.

Photo tip: If you arrive around noon, the harsh overhead light won't produce the glowy, ethereal photos you've seen on Instagram. The light is better in the afternoon, when the shadowy Subway is illuminated by reflected light from downstream canyon walls. But don't hang around too long. The rugged trail back gets progressively more dangerous as daylight fades.

⤚ WEST RIM TRAIL ⤙

SUMMARY Considered one of the best backpacks in Zion, the West Rim Trail passes through a fantastic range of landscapes. The trail starts among tall ponderosa pines and quaking aspen near Lava Point (p.255), then drops into a piñon-juniper forest with scattered views of West Zion's dramatic peaks. With each passing mile, the views get better. Six of the trail's eight campsites sit atop a lofty plateau overlooking dramatic, Seussian sandstone peaks. From the plateau the trail drops into a glorious expanse of sheer cliffs and rolling slickrock just west of Zion Canyon. The West Rim Trail ultimately intersects with the trail to Angels Landing, then descends to the floor of Zion Canyon. Although it's possible to hike the West Rim Trail in a single day, a two-day backpack gives you more time to relax and enjoy the scenery. Backpacking permits are required (p.14).

TRAILHEAD The West Rim Trail starts 3/4 of a mile southeast of Lava Point. Private hiking shuttles (p.14) often drop hikers off at Lava Point Campground, where you can use the toilet before you start hiking.

TRAIL INFO

RATING: Strenuous   **DISTANCE:** 14.2 miles

HIKING TIME: 1–2 days   **ELEVATION CHANGE:** 3,400 feet

West Rim Trail Description

TRAILHEAD The West Rim Trailhead is located off a dirt road just below Lava Point (p.255). It's worth stopping at Lava Point Campground to use the toilet. You can then stroll to Lava Point to enjoy the panoramic views. From the campground follow the spur trail 0.1 miles to the dirt road, then turn right and walk 0.7 miles to the trailhead. You'll soon reach a junction with the Wildcat Trail. Continue straight (south) across Horse Pasture Plateau.

SAWMILL SPRING JUNCTION (1 MILE) A spur trail leads to the first of three dependable springs on the West Rim Trail. The Zion wilderness desk posts which springs are currently flowing.

POTATO HOLLOW SPRING (5.2 MILES) After passing a series of pretty meadows along Horse Pasture Plateau, you'll reach a signed junction for Potato Hollow Spring. This is the last dependable water source before Cabin Spring. Backpackers should replenish their water here. Potato Hollow Spring is located off the spur trail to campsite 8.

TELEPHONE CANYON JUNCTION (6.8 MILES) After dipping up and down and passing several lovely viewpoints, the trail heads uphill to the West Rim. Before reaching the rim, the Telephone Canyon Trail veers left, offering a 1.8-mile shortcut to West (Cabin) Spring. Continue right along the scenic West Rim Trail, where campsites 2–6 are located. As the trail skirts the rim, you'll be treated to gorgeous views of dramatic sandstone peaks.

WEST (CABIN) SPRING (9.8 MILES) Towards the end of the West Rim, the trail descends into a grove of tall ponderosa pines. Near the southern junction with the Telephone Canyon Trail, a spur trail heads to West (Cabin) Spring. After replenishing your water supply, continue along the spur trail to an exposed lookout with stunning views (p.212).

Back on the trail, you'll descend the steep walls of Behunin Canyon, then curve around the base of Mount Majestic. Waves of bleached sandstone roll across the landscape. This is one of my favorite places in Zion. Eventually the trail ascends the eastern edge of Refrigerator Canyon where cairns (small rock piles) mark the sometimes faint trail.

SCOUT LOOKOUT (12.4 MILES) The West Rim Trail officially ends at Scout Lookout, where crowds line up for the final push to Angels Landing (p.174).

THE GROTTO (14.2 MILES) From The Grotto Shuttle Stop (#6) catch Zion's free shuttle back to civilization.

Hiking around the base of Mount Majestic

"Great West Canyon has marvelously colored slopes and side canyons, and from the rim, one may look down on a rolling sea of white sandstone brilliantly streaked with pink ... Great temples and buttes of varied architecture and coloring are isolated by narrow V-shaped canyons."

—LeRoy Jeffers, 1919

View from the West Rim

⊰ NORTHGATE PEAKS ⊱

SUMMARY Few trails in Zion offer so much scenery with so little elevation change. If you're traveling with children or not-so-strong hikers, Northgate Peaks is an excellent option. From the Wildcat Canyon Trailhead, follow the trail through a large meadow into a picturesque forest. After about one mile you'll reach the junction with the Connector Trail. Veer left and hike about 0.2 miles to the junction with the Northgate Peaks Trail. Turn right (south) and follow the trail to a signed junction. To the left, a spur trail drops into Russell Gulch, which empties into the Left Fork of North Creek. The spur trail is used by canyoneers to access The Subway (p.256), but you'll want to veer right and stay on the broad path to Northgate Peaks. After about 10 minutes you'll descend to a lava rock promontory with panoramic views. The twin Northgate Peaks frame a dramatic view of North Guardian Angel's shark fin profile, with the cascading cliffs of West Zion beyond.

TRAILHEAD The Wildcat Canyon Trailhead parking area is located off Kolob Reservoir Road, 16 miles north of the junction with Route 9 in the town of Virgin.

TRAIL INFO

RATING: Easy	**DISTANCE:** 4.4 miles, round-trip
HIKING TIME: 1–2 Hours	**ELEVATION CHANGE:** 100 feet

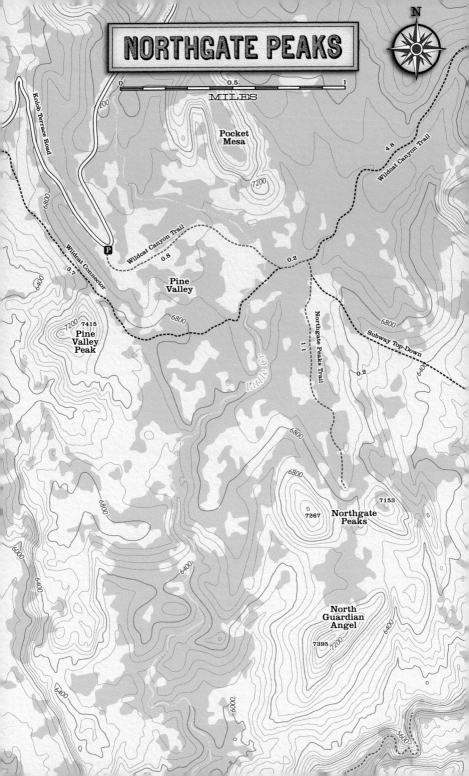

⚘ HOP VALLEY ⚘

SUMMARY The Hop Valley Trail runs from Kolob Terrace to Kolob Canyons (p.273), offering high elevation hiking and backpacking in a beautiful, over-looked part of the park. In summer, when crowds and temperatures are peaking in Zion Canyon, Hop Valley is a great escape. After an initial descent through Gambel oak, desert scrub and piñon/juniper forest, you'll stroll through long, flat Hop Valley, which is surrounded by beautiful sandstone walls. (Note: parts of Hop Valley do not belong to Zion and are open to cattle ranching, leading some locals to jokingly call the trail "Plop Valley.") Expect multiple stream crossings; hiking poles are helpful. At the northern end of Hop Valley, the trail descends to La Verkin Creek. Strong day hikers can visit Kolob Arch (p.282), 7.2 miles one way from the Hop Valley Trailhead. The trails below Hop Valley are particularly beautiful in late October when the leaves are changing.

TRAILHEAD The Hop Valley Trailhead is located in a roundabout parking area off Kolob Reservoir Road. The turnoff is 13 miles north of the junction with Route 9 in the small town of Virgin.

TRAIL INFO

RATING: Moderate

DISTANCE: 13 miles round-trip

HIKING TIME: 6–8 Hours

ELEVATION CHANGE: 1,050 feet

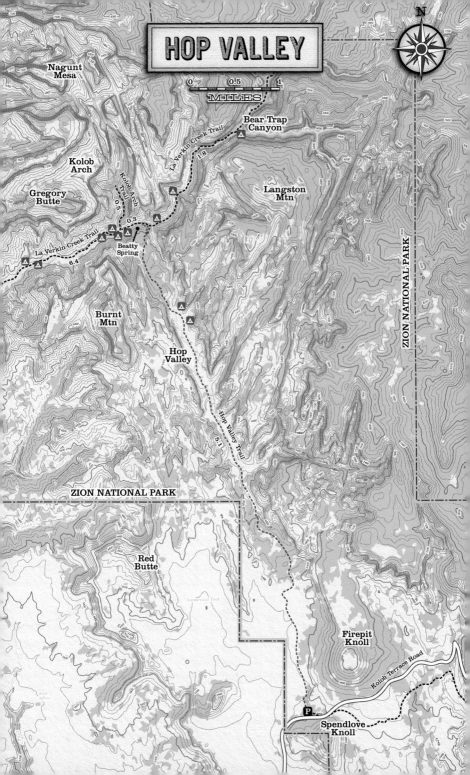

Hiking below Hop Valley

KOLOB CANYONS

LOCATED IN ZION'S remote northwest corner, Kolob Canyons offers Zion's signature sandstone cliffs with a fraction of the crowds. Just ten percent of Zion visitors make it to this part of the park, but those who do are rewarded with fabulous geology, great hiking, and unforgettable views from some of the highest driving roads in the park.

Start by checking in at the Kolob Canyons Visitor Center, which sits at the base of the Hurricane Cliffs—a dramatic incline that marks the western edge of the Colorado Plateau. From the visitor center, Kolob Canyons Road climbs above the flatlands of Harmony Valley and cuts into the rugged Kolob Canyons to the east. For the next several miles the road twists along a half-dozen "Finger Canyons," so-named because they extend like fingers across the landscape. You can stop and enjoy the views at numerous pullouts, but the real highlight is the road's dramatic last mile. The road ends at Kolob Canyons Lookout, a paved roundabout with terrific views of the towering sandstone cliffs.

One of the best ways to experience Kolob Canyons is to hike its trails. The Timber Creek Overlook Trail starts at Kolob Canyons Lookout and heads a half-mile to a beautiful viewpoint. For a longer, more challenging hike, consider Taylor Creek (p.280), which twists through a finger canyon en route to Double Arch Alcove. For an even longer hike follow the La Verkin Creek Trail (p.282) as it wraps seven miles around the base of the Kolob Canyons en route to Kolob Arch—one of the world's largest freestanding rock arches.

"Kolob" is a Mormon word named for the star closest to heaven, which is fitting for a region home to Zion's highest peak: Horse Ranch Mountain, which rises 8,926 feet above sea level just north of the finger canyons. Much of Kolob Canyons Road lies above 6,000 feet, making it distinctly cooler than the floor of 4,000-foot Zion Canyon. As a result, the hot summer months are one of the best times to visit Kolob Canyons. Autumn is also gorgeous, with colorful foliage along creeks and streams. Winter brings deep snow that sometimes closes the road. Spring snowmelt muddies the trails, but the upside is beautiful wildflowers. No matter when you visit Zion, there's always a good reason to visit Kolob Canyons.

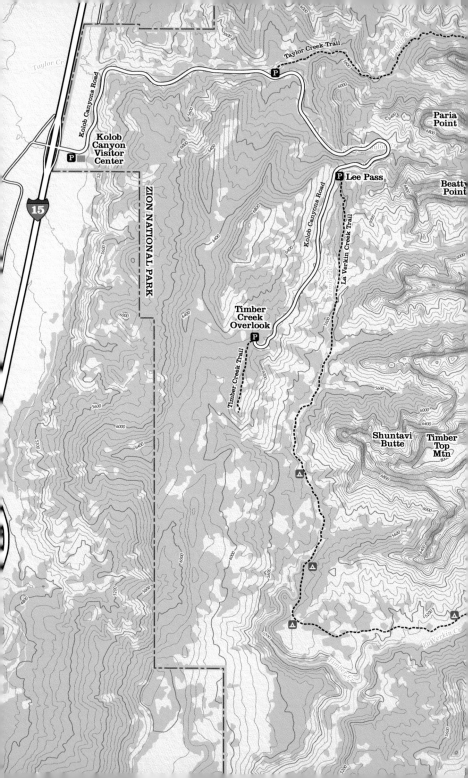

KOLOB CANYONS

N

Double Arch Alcove

N. Fork Taylor Cr.

Middle Fork Taylor Cr.

Buck Pasture Mtn

Nagunt Mesa

Death Point

Herbs Point

Bullpen Mtn

La Verkin Creek Trail

Bear Trap Canyon

Kolob Arch

Gregory Butte

Langston Mtn

Kolob Arch Trail

La Verkin Creek Trail

Hop Valley Trail

Burnt Mtn

Hop Valley

Kolob Canyons
Visitor Center

Kolob Canyons Visitor Center

The Kolob Canyons Visitor Center is located just off Interstate 15 at exit 40 (33 miles north of Saint George, 19 miles south of Cedar City). All visitors to Kolob Canyons are required to stop at the visitor center to show or purchase an entrance pass. You can also pick up wilderness permits for overnight hikes or browse the bookstore operated by The Zion Forever Project (p.39). The visitor center also has bathrooms, a water filling station, and outdoor displays that offer basic info about the region's geology and geography.

The Kolob Canyons Visitor Center is the only building in Zion National Park not located on Colorado Plateau (p.64). Technically, the visitor center is located in the Basin and Range Province, which stretches between the Colorado Plateau to the east and the Sierra Nevada Mountains to the west. The visitor center is located along the Hurricane Fault, which runs parallel to Interstate 15, stretches 150 miles, and marks the western boundary of the Colorado Plateau. As tectonic plates shifted over the past two million years, the Hurricane Cliffs, which rise directly behind the visitor center, were pushed up along the Hurricane Fault. This exposed 260 million-year-old Kaibab Limestone, one of the oldest rock layers in Zion. (Kaibab Limestone is also the youngest rock layer in Grand Canyon, where it caps both the North and South Rim.) The Hurricane Fault remains an active fault that occasionally triggers earthquakes. The last major earthquake, in 1992, measured 5.8 on the Richter scale. Future earthquakes are inevitable, and some could be much larger.

Timber Creek Overlook

Kolob Canyons Road heads five miles to Timber Creek Overlook, which offers panoramic views of the Finger Canyons. A sign near the railing points out individual peaks. To the southeast Shuntavi Point rises like a chubby missile below Timber Top Mountain. Many of the peaks to the north are based on Paiute words: Nagunt ("bighorn sheep") Mesa, Tucupit ("wildcat") Point, Paria ("elk") Point. Just left of Paria Point you can catch a glimpse of Horse Ranch Mountain, which at 8,926 feet is the tallest peak in Zion.

From Timber Creek Overlook the Kolob Finger Canyons line up like a military regiment. The striking western orientation of the canyons is due to faults (cracks) that formed in the ancient rock. Rain and runoff flowed west down the faults, forming streams that slowly eroded the landscape. As tectonic forces pushed up this region along the Hurricane Fault, the landscape tilted and stream erosion accelerated, carving deep canyons into the Navajo Sandstone. Each finger canyon is like a miniature Zion Canyon, with a wide mouth tapering to a narrow slot canyon in the upper reaches. But note how the Navajo Sandstone in Kolob Canyons is more reddish than in Zion Canyon. This red coloration is due to iron leaching down from overlying rock layers.

For even better views of the Finger Canyons follow the Timber Creek Overlook Trail a half-mile from the parking area to a beautiful viewpoint. To the southeast you can also see the stairstep plateaus of Kolob Terrace as they march towards Zion Canyon.

Timber Creek
Overlook

⚮ TAYLOR CREEK TRAIL ⌐

SUMMARY   Taylor Creek Trail is the best moderate hike in Kolob Canyons. The 2.5-mile trail, which parallels Taylor Creek as it flows through a narrow box canyon, ends at a striking location known as Double Arch Alcove (above). From the trailhead, wooden stairs descend to Taylor Creek. En route to the alcove you'll crisscross the creek over a dozen times. Hiking poles are helpful, particularly when the creek is running high. The trail ascends a relatively easy, consistent gradient. Along the way you'll pass Larson Cabin, built in 1930 by pig farmer Gustav Larson. A short distance later you'll pass Fife cabin, built in 1930 by goat farmer Arthur Fife. The trail ends at Double Arch Alcove, where two stone arches are stacked on top of each other. The lower arch formed due to erosion by seeping water. The upper arch formed along natural cracks in the rock. Stepping into the wavy, multicolored alcove feels like entering a Georgia O'Keeffe painting, while dark desert varnish (p.55) drips down like Jackson Pollock splatter.

TRAILHEAD   The trailhead is located 1.9 miles past the Kolob Canyons Visitor Center. Look for a paved parking area with toilets.

TRAIL INFO

RATING: Moderate

DISTANCE: 5 miles, round-trip

HIKING TIME: 4 hours

ELEVATION CHANGE: 450 feet

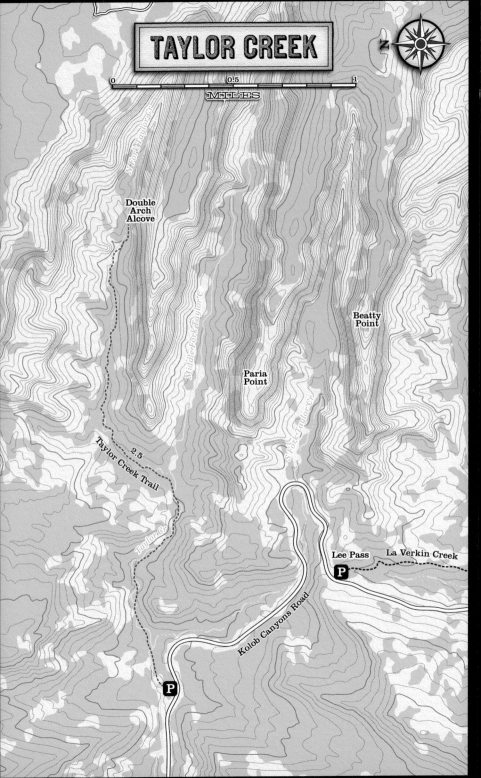

~❧ LA VERKIN CREEK TRAIL ❧~

SUMMARY   This gorgeous trail offers unparalleled views of Kolob's Finger Canyons as it heads to Kolob Arch (above). From Lee Pass (named for Mormon renegade John D. Lee, who hid out in this area after the 1857 Mountain Meadows Massacre), the trail drops to Timber Creek, which flows below Kolob Canyons Road. Near the southern tip of the Finger Canyons the trail cuts east along La Verkin Creek ("La Verkin" is a corruption of the Spanish *La Virgen*). About 6.5 miles past the trailhead, a 0.5-mile spur trail heads north to a viewpoint below Kolob Arch. Measuring nearly 300 feet long and 75 feet thick, Kolob Arch is one of the world's largest free-standing rock arches. It formed due to a geologic process called exfoliation where slabs of rock peel off like layers of an onion. For even more hiking continue along the La Verkin Creek Trail up to Bear Trap Canyon. Backpacking note: Camping is restricted to individual campsites along Taylor Creek and La Verkin Creek that must be reserved in advance.

TRAILHEAD   The La Verkin Creek Trail starts at Lee Pass, 3.6 miles from the Kolob Canyons Visitor Center.

TRAIL INFO

RATING: Moderate

DISTANCE: 14 miles, round-trip

HIKING TIME: 8 hours

ELEVATION CHANGE: 1,037 feet

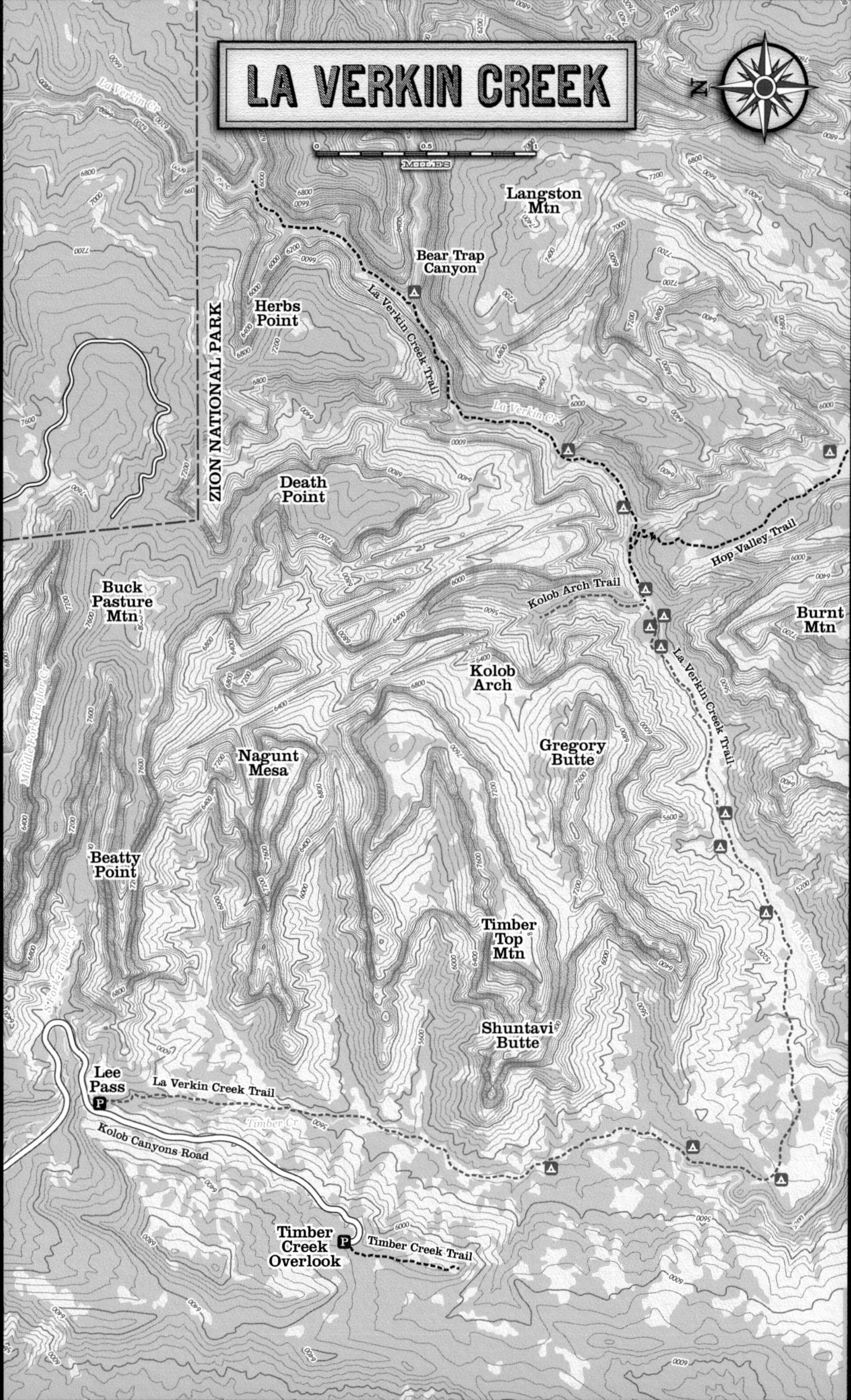

LA VERKIN CREEK

N

MILES
0   0.5   1

Langston Mtn

Bear Trap Canyon

La Verkin Creek Trail

Herbs Point

ZION NATIONAL PARK

La Verkin Cr.

Hop Valley Trail

Death Point

Kolob Arch Trail

Burnt Mtn

Buck Pasture Mtn

Kolob Arch

La Verkin Creek Trail

Gregory Butte

Nagunt Mesa

Beatty Point

Timber Top Mtn

Shuntavi Butte

Lee Pass

La Verkin Creek Trail

Kolob Canyons Road

Timber Cr.

Timber Creek Overlook

Timber Creek Trail

La Verkin Creek

Extraordinary Guides to Extraordinary National Parks

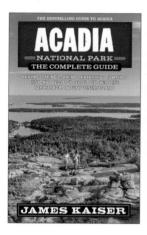

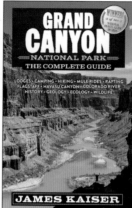

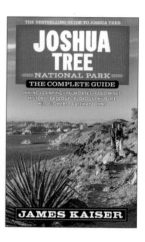

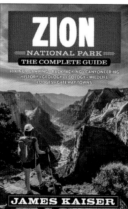

Need help customizing the perfect trip?

jameskaiser.com/travel-consulting